# The Lives of Jesus

# The Lives of Jesus

## The Greatest Story Never Told

### Eldon Peat

Amarna Books and Media
www.amarnabooksandmedia.com

ISBN: 978-0-9828951-3-9
ISBN-10: 0982895135

Cover image: Matthias Grünewald, *The Resurrection* from the *Isenheim Altarpiece*, c. 1515

# CONTENTS

# How This Book Came To Be

L ATE ONE EVENING in April of 1986, while seated at a type-writer working on a project, I began to fall into a very deep trance-like state. Although I became unaware of my surroundings, I was still capable of voluntary movement. I began to hear a voice speaking clearly and directly to me, and as it spoke I typed what the voice said:

*"Love casts out fear. That you shall see the effect of this shall be your life's work. Know that your master it is that speaks to you for I shall send words to your mouth that shall reach the sons of man throughout the world. The time of your purification is now at hand. Spend time with me at the turn of each day and I shall direct your hands. It is the work that you and I have begun since the beginning of time and shall now be completed. Turn to me in your hour of need and I shall be your comfort. It shall be for you to turn the hearts of all men unto their maker. This is your mission.*

*In meditation shall you set your feet before the altar of God the almighty. For as you are a Son of God, know that all men are so. I come to you so that you might know your holy purpose and fulfill your destiny here. Today we begin the Mystery of Man: that all might know their Source and forget the entanglements of the world and the flesh. Let your faith become as a rod of iron so that it may not bend to the wills and whims of others. Set you upon the path of righteousness and your eyes shall be opened to all miracles.*

*Let this be the preface to your book of enlightenment. For as you enter the path of awakening, others shall want to know the way that is open to them also.*

*All power is yours. Look inside so that you may see what riches God has in store for you. Know that the world is but a world of false needs and that your God inside meets all wants. [...]*

*Think not that you are unworthy of the task that is before you for I have chosen you to convey this message. This is to be a handbook for the awakening, so that all may have a guide. Before your time is out all men must come to this point so that time may have an end. The endless round of birth and death, which some call karma, is to have an end in the world of love and grace, which means the coming of all men to their Christ spirit."*

The voice continued, and instructed me to sit at my typewriter every evening at the same time to receive more material. Although I was disturbed by this phenomenon, I kept my "appointment," sat down at the typewriter, relaxed myself, and the voice came back.

This time it began to dictate what appeared to be a long manuscript. It began with a complete table of contents, chapter by chapter, and proceeded to dictate an introduction. At the end of that evening's session, in a normal waking state I read what I had typed: it appeared to be a biography of Jesus.

The writing style of the book was not mine. It discussed topics in an authoritative way—topics which I have never studied. The voice encouraged me to verify facts, and I checked many unfamiliar and seemingly suspicious ideas in the manuscript with current references. Surprisingly, most of the facts checked out. Where there were lapses in the research materials, there were often scholarly conjectures that corresponded with the manuscript's ideas. Moreover, the dictated material made references to other chapters within the text—chapters which were not actually dictated and "channeled" until several years later.

For after "channeling" about a third of the manuscript, I became quite disturbed at what was happening and put the text away. I realized that the import of what I was typing was sensational and potentially incendiary, and I began to doubt my own sanity. I did not want to continue, even though I became convinced that I was indeed in my right mind.

Several years later, after much thought and on very good advice, I decided to see if I could receive the rest of the material. By this time I had a computer, and once again I sat at the keyboard, relaxed my concentration, and asked—whoever it was—to continue the book.

Without hesitation, the voice began to dictate the rest of the material beginning at exactly the point where I had quit years before. Where the early parts made references to later chapters, those chapters were now dictated intact, often with references back to earlier chapters.

The remainder of the book was dictated, exactly following the scheme outlined in the table of contents. During the dictation of this book, I was only provided with one personal session in which I was allowed to ask questions, and relevant portions of that session follow:

**"Q: What is the source of this material?**

*A: This has been given in same. You shall be the channel for its expression. Be you my servant in this. Have faith, and believe in this miracle. Have you not asked for miracles, and do you now want to deny the coming of same? I do keep my promises which I have made.*

**Q: I cannot believe that this is happening to me.**

*A: O, ye of little faith. Take this, and profit by it, so that all who are your brothers and sisters may profit by it in turn. Time is running out for this world, and we must quicken the return to the Father. It was for this purpose that I came two thousand years ago, and since that time much chaos has come. It is time for a cleansing of this world, as has happened in times past; yet if men may change their minds, this, too, may be averted or softened. The earth is a child of God as well, with its own intelligence; you exist almost as a parasite upon its surface. In its time, it will cleanse itself. That time is near at hand. As I charged you many times, you must spread the news to all men of the way that is open to them, that which I have shown you.*

*Let the fact that I am come to give you this book be as a sign that I am still with you, to show you the way. For indeed, I have conquered death, and am alive! I no longer have the need for a body as a means of communication. I have chosen you, not now, but long ago. You have chosen to postpone your fulfillment of our covenant until this time, not through sin or error, but out of the knowledge that this time was to come.*

## Q: Are other sources involved in dictating this work?

*A: The Holy Spirit is the Source of all Knowledge. Seek no further than this. For the Spirit and I have become one, and this is the pattern for you all. Let this be a message for this book.*

*We have chosen you to convey this message, and have seen to it that you are prepared for its communication. You are not so enamored of one set of beliefs that you shall bend what will be given you unto one form or another. Even now as you receive these words there is a doubt and skepticism that wonders of its miraculous source. Did I not promise to be with you always? I know the temptations of the world, as well as its condemnation. Did you not see how little that mattered to me in the great demonstration of the power of God? For was I not condemned and killed, and did I not reveal that death to be a ridiculous illusion?*

*Even then did you doubt me. Yet we do have a mission to fulfill, you and I. I have not forsaken you even though you have often turned your back on me.*

*The time is now ripe for a rebirth of the spirit within you and within all men in the Sonship of God. This must come about before the millennium of yore. Men must open their hearts to God and think not of themselves only. Many are in need of enlightenment, and are hungering for such truth. Many sources are available to men but the truest is a search within the self for answers to the questions that have been raised since the dawn of Man. This way is also the narrow way, which few can enter. Yet it is also the best way, for it is indeed the only way through which Man may return to the infinite. Channels of communication are being opened to men, if they will heed them. Many such as this one will pledge themselves to carry forth the word to their brothers, and do so in service of God and fellow men. The times to come ahead are fraught with peril for the bodies of men, but can be overcome or transformed through unification of spirit. This must be conducted through one individual at a time, as each one makes his choice for God. Many attempts to organize such a mass conversion are the result of power and ego. The awakening of the spirit is a highly personal matter, and cannot and should not be attempted in masses. Yet when the spirit is reborn, then the masses shall know."*

I present the book exactly as it was dictated to me. I offer no further explanation or judgment about the material. Its source is still a mystery to me, and I do not necessarily endorse any or all of its hypotheses. My role is to remain the anonymous messenger who fulfills his obligation.

# PREFACE

THERE IS NO DOUBT as to the existence of the historical personage known as Jesus. This volume will not attempt to settle this issue. What we are going to set forth is the record of the historical events in that person's life which have, to date, gone unrecorded by any existing document. In the past much had been written about this person, but the writings have been "declassified", declared uncanonical, and, often, burned.

The author of this book is not the true author of this source material. He is being fed information directly from the Akashic records which has hitherto been reported erroneously. By the end of this century *[editor's note: this book was begun in 1986]*, material not unlike the Dead Sea Scrolls and the Nag Hammadi library will come to light confirming the accuracy of these writings. These writings are being published pseudonymously so as to protect the life and family of the scribe, whose identity will remain concealed until such time as the general public can accept the theses put forth herein.

Much psychological preparation has been given to the recipient so that this material can be transmitted, but it must be clearly stated that the scribe, about whom no more shall be stated after this paragraph, is neither saint nor angel, but a mere mortal who has been elected as the vehicle for transmission. He is not a cleric or divine, but is one who, in another life, knew the Master known as Jesus in the flesh and has been brought to this task to convey this astonishing story to you, the reader.

Perhaps the first hurdle for many modern Christians to cross is one that has been touched upon in the preceding paragraph. Reincarnation is one of the oldest beliefs held on earth, and, while it is not to be taken as an actual fact, it is but a representation of a much deeper reality that can only be communicated to modern believers and skeptics in symbolic terms. Reincarnation was the cornerstone of the gnostic beliefs of the Essenes, the sect to which Jesus belonged. It is this oft-maligned doctrine that has been mistranslated in the Scriptures as "resurrection".

For centuries, the Christian faith has centered on the resurrection of Jesus, the "only Son of God". Wars have been fought, boundaries redrawn, countless lives lost, and rivers of blood shed for this mythical Jesus. This person did exist, but not in the form of popular belief. This is his biography. Any reader who is about to shout "blasphemy" or "sacrilege" should abandon his or her reading right now. This text can and should only be approached by those with open and flexible minds, or at the very least those wishing to increase the flexibility of their minds and systems of belief.

# PART ONE

The Life of the Historical Jesus

# CHAPTER ONE

# Akhnaton and Moses

Y'SHUA BEN YUSEF WAS BORN in what is generally regarded as 4 B.C. or, to remove the sectarian notion of current scholarship, B.C.E. (It is this notation that we will use.) His father, Yusef ben Y'shua (his father also held the name of Y'shua or Joshua, so the child was named for his grandfather) was not, as common legend would have it, a carpenter. He was, indeed, not of low birth or social stature. He was the son of a wealthy merchant who traded in spices and carpets with the Far East. The family home was in Jerusalem, and was opulent. In addition, the family had a second home, what would be called today a "country house", in Capernaum, near the Sea of Galilee.

Y'shua was normal when born. No star attended his birth. He was born in his father's house, not in a manger or stable. We shall address the folklore involved in this transformation in a later chapter. His mother was named Miriam, and she was of a family of lesser means, yet the family of Miriam was of the priestly caste of the Essenes, to which Yusef's family belonged. The marriage was considered advantageous for Miriam's family, since it elevated her financial and social status, but for Y'shua the father of Yusef, the marriage was one that honored his family, since Miriam was of the highest level of spiritual teachers of the Essenes.

This does not mean that the birth of the son of this union was without significance. The Essenes believed, as noted above, in reincarnation, and they knew that the child to be born to Miriam was, in fact, to be the Messiah. This is where popular religion and the historical facts of the Essenes cross.

The Essenes were a sect given to a radical reinterpretation of Judaism as it existed at that time. Judea, the land of Israel, was under Roman domination, and though Judaism was the religion of the people, there was nothing like agreement among the people. Every small group had its own teacher or rabbi, and each group held radically different beliefs. What was common to most of these sects, however, was the belief that they were in the "last times" and that the arrival of the Messiah was imminent.

Today we have heard the word "Messiah" used in reference to Jesus, but in the context of Roman-occupied Judea, it had a radically different meaning. Most sects looked for a Messiah to come, as prophesied in what we now call the Old Testament, to deliver the people of Israel from bondage. Now we must digress a bit into the history of the Jews.

The Jews, as we know them today, were a people in exile from their homelands, captured by the Mesopotamian general Cyrus or Khairos (not the later, historically prominent Cyrus of Persia but a minor temporal tyrant) and sold into slavery. Some of these facts are, and will appear to be, in direct contradiction to the Old Testament scriptures. We shall see, in succeeding chapters, how these texts have been radically edited and altered over the centuries. Some of the books accepted as canonical are, indeed, forgeries.

Khairos found his Semitic captives to be of little use to him, as they were nomadic, hardy and self-sufficient desert wanderers, fanatic in their devotion to a bloody, vengeful deity they called Yahweh (Jehovah). Khairos needed agricultural workers and metalsmiths, so, never a man to miss a bargain, he sold these captives to the Pharaoh of Egypt, who was widely thought among Mediterranean peoples to be a gullible fool.

This Pharaoh was Akhnaton, husband of Nefrtiti. Akhnaton had abandoned the multiple-god religion of the earlier Pharaohs, moved the capital of Egypt from Thebes to the desert, where he founded a new city called Amarna. He was, in short, a radical. Akhnaton was, however, a great mystic and seer, spontaneously clairvoyant and clairaudient, and able to intuit the ancient laws of the planet.

Akhnaton drew from his clairvoyant perceptions that there was, indeed, not a single man-like god or several gods, but a powerful, intelligent life force that shaped the universe. This force was beyond human knowing, yet permeated every bit of matter in the universe. Akhnaton learned that this superior intelligence, which took the form of a symbolic god or set of gods, was the same in every culture and expressed itself in nothing but loving ways. As Akhnaton believed, this force was the "glue" that shaped matter, and existed everyplace and noplace at once.

This awareness, as Akhnaton realized, is the basis for all world religions and is personified and interpreted by each culture according to its ability to grasp such an abstract concept.

Long before Khairos sold the Jews to Akhnaton, Akhnaton's queen (and half-sister) Nefrtiti had a vision, whereby she knew that the Jews were to be sold, and urged her husband to buy them. She learned in her vision that of all the people in the Near East, the Jews had come closest to Akhnaton's concept of a divinity in their conception of Yahweh, and she knew that if the Jews could come to the court of Akhnaton at Amarna, their two systems of belief could be merged, and a new concept of "God" could be introduced to the world.

So, when the seemingly worthless Jews were put on the slave market (as happened often in those days of conquest), Akhnaton rushed to buy them, and settled them in his own city of Amarna. He treated them with great kindness and respect, which was unheard of in dealing with slaves or prisoners of war. This was one of the reasons Akhnaton was considered a fool by the warlike general-kings of the Middle East.

Akhnaton spent days and days in consultation with the leaders of the Jews, who are the figures passed down to history and legend as Moses and Aaron. These two brothers were themselves visionaries. Aaron had been a priest of another religion, one based on moon-bull worship (which has been passed down in legend as the "golden calf" episode in Exodus) when his brother had a vision not unlike that of Akhnaton, a vision of a single unifying intelligence that permeated the universe. Crafty and politic, Aaron helped his mystical brother shape a new mythology that melded with the old, and together they forged a new slate of rules of conduct for their tribes, codified in ten succinct beliefs. A simpler, more elegant code for human behavior has never been set forth.

These two brothers were given this code as they sat meditating on top of a mountain, so the popular story of Moses on the mountain receiving the tablets from God is, in fact, what did happen, rendered into symbolic terms that the other members of the tribes could understand.

The meeting of these brothers with Akhnaton was a true melding of sensibilities, and in their discourse many subjects were explored. (It should be noted that Moses and Aaron objected strongly to what they considered the incestuous marriage of Akhnaton and Nefrtiti, though the issue never came between them and was dismissed as a difference in cultures.) Moses became a favorite at Akhnaton's court, and these two, Moses and Akhnaton, planned a way to disseminate their findings throughout the world, by sending groups of "missionaries" across the Near East with copies of discourses that were written by Akhnaton and Moses together with Aaron, as well as more ancient texts held in the library of Amarna.

Before this plan could be put into effect, however, a rival Egyptian faction, opposed to Akhnaton's rule, mounted a great army and tried to storm the city of Amarna. Since Akhnaton was a ruler of peace, he did not have sufficient armies to defend his city and, as the siege was raised, could barely hold the city of Amarna defensively. The many onslaughts of the rival army have become, again in folklore, the seven plagues, since the enemies of Akhnaton tried any kind of attack they could imagine to weaken Akhnaton's hold on his desert city.

Moses suggested to Akhnaton that the Jews be offered to the rival Pharaoh's army (this Pharaoh was Tut-Amon, father of the famed but ineffectual Tut-Ankh-Amon), since they were, for all intents and purposes, tradable slaves. Akhnaton was unwilling to part with his treasured allies, but Moses prevailed. Between them, though, they hatched a plan. Akhnaton refused to yield his "City of God" to the "barbaric" forces of Tut-Amon. He would release the Jews to Tut-Amon, but the Jews were to send men to open the floodgates of the dam Akhnaton had built on the Nile that fed water to Amarna. Even though the city of Amarna would be lost in the rush of water through the formerly arid valley, the armies of Tut-Amon, encamped further down in the valley, would be drowned, and Moses and his people, situated in a "prison camp" on higher ground, could be saved. Moses was to lead his people back to Judea through the desert wastelands, and continue the work he and Akhnaton had agreed upon.

It does not take much imagination to recognize the mythical crossing of the Red Sea by Moses and the Israelites, by which the evil Pharaoh and his armies were drowned. What Moses and Aaron learned from Akhnaton, and took from Egypt, was a new concept of a just and loving god, unlike the cruel Yahweh. Despite the visionary dreams of Akhnaton, his concept of that same God-force drowned with the city of Amarna, and Egypt returned to the polytheistic religion of the Ptolemies.

What Moses and his people carried with them, however, were many of the sacred scrolls from the library of Amarna, hidden in a gold casket, which was eventually placed in the Temple of Solomon in Jerusalem: the Ark of the Covenant.

The Essenes, awaiting the birth of their Messiah, had divined the many prior incarnations of their coming prophet, and one of them was, not surprisingly, Akhnaton. Also in this long string of incarnations, which had brought this entity to a state nearing spiritual perfection, was as Joseph, or Yusef, of the Old Testament tales (most of which are as mythical as the account of Moses in Egypt).

Just as Moses was thought to have delivered the Jews from "bondage" in Egypt, so for most Jews in Roman-occupied Judea, the Messiah would be a strong military leader to remove the tyranny of Roman domination. The Essenes expected a "Messiah" of a totally different sort, for the revolution they expected was of an inner, spiritual dimension.

# CHAPTER TWO

# Judea Under the Romans

J UDEA UNDER THE ROMANS was merely an obscure province, a necessary stronghold in a vast empire, but one that was more troublesome than it was profitable. Jerusalem was a center for many trade routes with Roman settlements in Europe, the Middle East and India. One of the most cosmopolitan cities of the Roman Empire, it was also the least tolerant of Roman rule.

Since Jews honored Jerusalem as the shrine of David and Solomon, this was the spiritual center as well as the cultural and political center of Israel. Many believed at that time that the nation of Israel was in fact a genuine nation and not a spiritual one, and that the Romans had no business trying to run the affairs of Judea. Because the Jews were ready to fight for their own independence at almost any provocation, the Romans had installed a puppet king, so that they could say that the Jews were ruled by one of their own, and that the Romans were merely the administrators of justice.

In fact, the puppet-king, Herod the Great, was not even of royal blood, but was put on the throne in a huge, Roman-generated campaign of propaganda to make most Jews believe that Herod was the rightful king of Judea. Most of the more affluent families knew better.

The royal blood of David and Solomon coursed through the veins of most of the nobler families, including those of Miriam and Yusef. In fact, many families traced their bloodlines back to the line of kings set in motion by David. The ancient prophecies of the Old Testament said that the Messiah would be born of the House of David. This was not particularly exclusive, for at the time of the birth of Y'shua, there were literally hundreds who could claim that birthright.

Not surprisingly, a number of Messiahs had arisen, all mightily armed to overthrow not only the Romans, but their puppet (and false) monarchy. Also not surprisingly, most of these insurrections were quashed by the superior Roman army and the perpetrators put to death in the Romans' favorite means of capital punishment, crucifixion.

The many radical sects whose leaders were so crucified by the Romans would then scatter, so as to avoid guilt—and possible execution—by association, but the public deaths of so many martyrs only fired the flames of revolution against Rome.

The Judean economy was almost crippled by Roman taxation, and many of the merchants—who controlled the priests of the Temple of Solomon—were themselves looking for ways to end the Romans' tyrannical control of all trading and seaports. While the underprivileged fought in the streets, the wealthier and more influential families sought to bring a diplomatic and political end to the domination of Caesar Augustus's forces.

To make matters worse, the line of Caesars had proclaimed themselves gods, which was blasphemy in the eyes of the Yahweh-worshipping priests. Augustus was canny enough to play down this fact in the display of his image in and around Jerusalem, and was made to seem a mortal, yet the posting of that very image was itself a violation of a scriptural law prohibiting "graven images of Gods"—a holdover from the theology of Akhnaton. Akhnaton taught Moses that since the deity he worshiped was in everything, it was impossible to create an image, or even a symbol, that would begin to signify the immensity of this loving intelligence.

The family of Yusef, like the family of Miriam, belonged to a mystical sect called the Essenes, as has been noted above. The Essenes taught—and fervently believed—that no matter who was in control of Israel's lands, the true revolution and escape from tyranny was to "go within" and find the indwelling God. The Essenes had carried forth the doctrines forged by Moses, Aaron, and Akhnaton, had been in communication with sages in India and China, and were conversant with the thoughts of Gautama Buddha, Kung-Fu Tze (Confucius) and Lao Tzu.

It is generally thought today that all of the major world religions grew independently of each other, but because of the wide-ranging trade routes of the Roman Empire, many of which were used by Jewish merchants, there was considerable cross-cultural communication. Miriam's brother, Yusef, known to us through the New Testament references as Joseph of Arimithea, was one such merchant. His personal passion for the study of comparative religions caused him to plan his trade routes in such a way that he could converse with the leaders of many ancient mystery schools around the world.

Yusef of Arimithea (so called because his storehouses were in that town, even though he lived most of the time in Jerusalem) was in constant contact with the Greek mystery schools that taught the Eleusinian mysteries, with the oracles at Delphi and Ephesus, with many sects of the followers of Buddha in India, and with the Celtic mystery schools of Ireland, Scotland, and, particularly, what is now Glastonbury in England.

Although the great library at Alexandria had been destroyed, many of the ancient documents had been collected by men such as Yusef of Arimithea, and the Essene library near Jerusalem was a particularly extensive one. The Essene community was one of far-reaching vision, particularly in the course of political events in the Middle East in the first century B.C.E. They possessed an historical overview unsurpassed in the Middle East and knew, for instance, of the destruction of the Temple of Solomon in 66 C.E. long before that event came to pass.

The Diaspora that followed that event was part of a long-known divine plan to scatter the Akhnaton-Moses doctrine (a portion of which is in Appendix II) across the known world. Though the Jews have suffered as a result of this Diaspora, their mystical, cabalistic knowledge has pervaded the entire world and is, in fact, in the process of transforming the face of the entire culture where so many lives were lost during the Second World War.

It may be considered that so many millions of Jews sent into spirit by Hitler's demonic forces have lingered in Eastern Europe and brought about the transformations of the democratic revolutions of 1989-90 and beyond, bringing the Soviet Union to its knees in the face of the almighty's need for democracy. When this truth is revealed, the concentration camps that stand in ruins will become places of pilgrimage, for indeed the six million and more whose lives were taken must be revered and honored, for many of them remain in spirit and will find no need to reincarnate as long as their sacrifice is honored by those in flesh.

All of this and more was foretold by the Essenes, perhaps one of the most remarkable communities of seers in the history of the world. At present, little is known of their activities; in fact, until the discoveries of the Dead Sea Scrolls in 1947 and the Nag Hammadi libraries, their existence was known to very few, mostly historians who have read Josephus's histories of The Jewish War, a description of that pivotal event that happened in 66-70 C.E.

It was, in fact, in 70 C.E. that the historical Jesus, Y'shua ben Yusef, passed into spirit. He was indeed crucified under Pontius Pilate, the Roman proconsul, in 34 C.E., when he was thirty-eight years of age, and, although the actual significance of the event has been distorted throughout history, he survived that crucifixion, appeared again to his friends and relatives, and lived to a ripe old age for his time, dying at the age of seventy-four prior to the siege of Masada.

History has recorded some of these events, and they have subsequently been denied by religious zealots, chief of which is Paul, known as Saul of Tarsus. A later section of this book will deal with Paul's distortions of history and his (very compelling) reasons for such distortions. The dangers of revealing the truth have been felt by those who have tried to bring them forth in the face of orthodox mythology, and many have given their lives as "heretics". This line of "heretics" reaches from the Arians at the Council of Nicaea in 325 C.E. through the Cathars, or Albigensians, through the inquisition in Spain to death threats against both Nikos Kazantzakis and Martin Scorsese, the author of the book and director of the film, respectively, of *The Last Temptation of Christ*, which attempted to pave the way for a radical reinterpretation of a very powerful myth.

This powerful myth of the Christ was, in fact, partially perpetrated by the Essenes themselves. Their studies in comparative religions and mythologies, aided in part by their chief patron, Yusef of Arimithea, the brother of Miriam, made it imperative for them to cast Miriam's son, Y'shua, in the classical mold of the Christ, which appears in the mythologies of many cultures.

One of the commonest myths, as pervasive as the belief in reincarnation, is that of the hero who suffers, dies, and is reborn after three days in the underworld. This hero-myth was common in Mediterranean cultures since the Bronze Age, and its power was that which created the harvest sacrifice. The transformation of human culture from nomadic to agrarian made people aware of the cycles of nature, by which growing things seem to die, give their lives, as it were, at harvest time, appear to go "underground" during the winter, and are "reborn" at springtime.

A common Bronze Age harvest ritual was to take a leader of the tribe and slaughter him, chop him to pieces, and bury him in the field. The sprouting of crops in the spring was traced directly to this ritual, barbaric though it may seem to modern sensibilities. It was a matter of great honor to be chosen to be this sacrifice, and this myth has untold resonance as a racial memory of mankind.

Early Christian celebrations, by the way, followed this cycle. The "crucifixion" of the Hero-Christ was celebrated in the winter, and his resurrection in the spring, with little regard for the historical events of the crucifixion of Y'shua. This was when more attention was paid to mythology than historicity.

Though many later peoples, including the Jews, no longer practiced human sacrifice, animals became the surrogate sacrifice to the angry god Yahweh. Both Moses and Aaron practiced ritual sacrifice, and we only have to go back as far as Abraham (or Abram, as he is also known), the father of the Jews, to see a direct tale of human sacrifice acted out. You will recall that Abram was about to sacrifice his son Isaac when the voice of Yahweh stopped him. This is, in mythological terms, the time in history when human sacrifice was replaced by animal sacrifice.

Through their contact with Akhnaton, however, Moses and Aaron were convinced of the futility and waste of sacrificing even animals to a bloody and angry god. Akhnaton showed them how the harvest-spring cycle was in itself nature's sacrifice and rebirth, so that the ritual act of sacrifice was unnecessary. What Akhnaton insisted upon, however, was the ritual blessing of the killing of animals for meat, and it was through this influence that the customs of kosher killing were brought into Judaism.

Yet the myth of the savior-hero, whose life must be given so that the tribe may live, persisted, and was wedded to the life of Y'shua, since, until his time, animal sacrifice was pervasive. The melding of myths, wisely seen by the Essenes as necessary to stop the senseless killing of sacrificial animals, has instead been distorted into a strange and perverted theology, as later chapters will explain.

Many people do not understand some of the ramifications of Jesus, in the Gospels, turning the money-lenders out of the Temple of Solomon (which would, in itself, have been a criminal act enough to bring about the arrest of Y'shua). In addition to his outrage over the desecration of a holy site, both from without and within (the corrupt priestly caste of Jerusalem was in the employ of Rome), Jesus wished to put an end to the senseless killing of innocent animals for sacrifice when so many of the poor of Judea went without food. Hence, it was a political as well as a religious action, a radical form of civil disobedience, as it were.

It is impossible to evaluate the life of Jesus, or Y'shua (from here on, we will generally refer to him as Jesus) without placing his life in an historical context. Because his life and actions have been elevated to the level of mythology, the actual achievements of the man have been overlooked by history. Many attempts have indeed been made to discount the actual achievement of the man Jesus, which are, in themselves, more miraculous than those of Jesus the mythological Son of God.

# CHAPTER THREE

# The Birth of Jesus

THE STAR OF DAVID, which was reported to have hovered over Bethlehem at the birth of Jesus, was not physically apparent over the skies of Judea in 4 B.C.E. The six-pointed star is, in fact, a very ancient mystical symbol for the convergence of heavens and earth. One triangle, with its base resting on the ground, converges with another triangle, its base resting on the firmament above, thus:

The great pyramids of Egypt were never meant as tombs, as has been commonly thought. They were tombs of a sort, used by the Mystery Schools of Thebes for initiation rites, which shall be limned in detail below. Their symbolism, which persists on the back of the American dollar bill to this date, is that of the earth-bound yearning towards Heaven. This does not mean that Heaven is in the skies, for that is merely the symbol. A more accurate image has been added to the picture of the pyramid on the dollar: at the apex of the pyramid is the inner-seeing eye of Horus, the "third eye" with which we hope to see into our own true natures. It should be remembered that many of the founding fathers of the United States were members of a mystical Masonic sect.

Until the time of the birth of Jesus, man was earthbound, yearning for the greater mystical knowledge of the "heavens", yet unable to reach beyond his earthly self. Akhnaton made such an attempt to transcend materialism, to "bring the Heavens into the common clay of man" (see Appendix II from the treatise by Akhnaton and Moses on the merging of heaven and earth), but failed when the priestly orthodoxy, conservative in the extreme, crushed his reform movement.

Astrology has been debased and cheapened in our modern era, but in the time of the Essenes, as it was in Egypt, observation of the stars was looked upon as a portent of great events on Earth. Until that time, only the earthbound pyramid represented man's strivings on earth. Through their own astrological observation of the stars and their mystical revelations, the Essenes were aware that a new era was about to come over the earth, in which mankind could become more aware of the universal mysteries, a merging, as it were, of "Heaven" and Earth.

So, even though the "Star of Bethlehem" did not actually appear in the skies, it was an inner symbol revealed to many mystics of the Middle East. This revelation of the Essenes was confirmed when three powerful astrologers, one from India, one from Arabia, and one from Africa, were compelled to travel to Jerusalem in 4 B.C.E. Again, they have survived in legend as the three Magi, come to Bethlehem.

Because the Jews had adopted this symbol of the merging triangles as the "Star of David", its appearance in the clairvoyant visions signified that mankind was about to enter a new age of awareness, in which the spiritual and the fleshly interpenetrated.

In Yoga, the body is believed to contain seven centers of energy, called chakras. The spiritual energy of the body, the kundalini, which is symbolized as a coiled serpent, lies dormant in the pelvis until a spiritual awakening sends this energy coursing up the body, filling each chakra as it rises. Each chakra is symbolized by a different image, and the third, the solar plexus, happens to be that of the six-pointed star, the "Star of David".

So you may see that when the Essenes and the other mystery school communities of the Near East envisioned such a star, they realized that a new awareness of spirituality was about to begin, and that symbol of energy rushing into a new center was the six-pointed star, the star of the Jews, with its center being Bethlehem... the City of David.

Jesus was not born in Bethlehem, as previously stated, but in Jerusalem. The birth in Bethlehem is, again, a powerful symbol, for through the bloodlines of both of his parents, Jesus was a descendant of David. Here we encounter one of the perplexing curiosities of the New Testament. Since these documents are a skillful mingling of myth, image, metaphysical treatise, and historical biography, heavily edited through the ages, we find the Gospels contain many contradictions. Since much emphasis is put on the divinity of Jesus in Matthew, Mark and Luke, his mother Mary (Miriam) is impregnated with the spirit of Yahweh, yet, without explanation, much is also made of the parentage of Jesus through his biological father, Yusef or Joseph, as well as through Mary.

Jewish tradition only traces bloodlines through the mother, yet two elaborate (and contradictory) genealogies are given in Matthew and Luke from David through Joseph to Jesus, even though we are told that Joseph was not the father of the child, but Mary's consort, she being a virgin and conceiving of the Holy Spirit. Why should this be?

The fact is that a myth common to many Mediterranean cultures has been wedded to the very real need to prove that Jesus was a descendant of David on both sides. If Yusef (Joseph) was not the biological father of Jesus, there is no need for such elaborate genealogies. Indeed, if Miriam conceived by the Divine, what need would there be to trace her own pedigree?

For the Jews, especially in those troubled times, the Messiah who would lead them out of bondage was to be of the line of David, a man, not a demi-god, so it was important that both parents be of the House of David, and they were.

Miriam's parents were both of the Essene priesthood. Unlike other orthodoxies of the time, the Essenes elevated both men and women to the priesthood, and many Essene rites were performed by married couples who were both priests. Priests of the Essene brotherhood were consecrated and anointed by their spouses, who carried equal spiritual weight in the community. While some of the Essene elders voluntarily practiced celibacy after a certain time of service in the priesthood, they remained married to their spouses. These facts will be of great significance in the life of Jesus, who was a practicing Essene.

Miriam's parents, then, were both priests. Her marriage to Yusef was arranged, as was the custom of the time, but only because these two were spiritually and psychologically compatible, both being of loving natures and devout in their beliefs. Moreover, they were both of the House of David, and, while the Essenes arranged many marriages in these families, many of whom claimed bloodlines of the ancient kings, Miriam and Yusef were told in ceremonial visions that they were to bear the Messiah.

Here we uncover another mysterious reference in the "accepted" Gospels. While Jesus was supposedly of divine birth, Mary and Joseph are recorded as having brought forth other children, six, in fact: Jacob ("James"), Jude, Miriam (named for her mother), Ruth, Simon, and Joses. Did these children treat their brother Jesus as a half-brother?

The beliefs of the Essenes may help to solve this mystery, for they taught that all conceptions were a divine miracle, a true manifestation of spirit into matter. Moreover, they taught that the spirit to be born actually helped to choose its own parents. The leader of the Essene community, Yanuf, and his wife Esther, co-celebrants of the Essene rites, while in deep trance states, were in communion with this powerful spirit that was to be incarnated as Jesus, who "arranged" the marriage of Miriam and Yusef and communicated it to the Essenes.

The Essenes were, surprisingly, skeptical of many of Yanuf's prophecies, at least until they were confirmed. The arrival of the three astrologers, who came to study and live at the Essene community at Qumran, confirmed the prophecy of the Messiah. They arrived individually within a week of one another, each claiming to have been compelled by a powerful dream in which a shining spirit told them to travel to Jerusalem and study with the Essenes for a year. They each, individually, consulted astrological charts, and confirmed that a peculiar convergence of planetary forces was indeed taking place.

Hence, the three Magi, or wise men, did travel to the birthplace of Jesus, and were actually present at the wedding of Miriam and Yusef, staying through the time that the child was born. They would have stayed longer, except that Herod, the King of the Jews, was scourging all foreigners from the area.

The Essenes were known throughout the Middle East as among the most hospitable of sects, a fact noted by the Jewish-Roman historian Josephus: "Their houses were open to all travelers, regardless of origin, race or belief. What's more, they expected no payment for the keep of their visitors." The three Magi, however, came to study with the Essenes, and insisted that the community take the expensive gifts and essences they brought. These, of course, have found their way into legend as the gifts of the Magi.

The symbolic references have been lost, however: frankincense and myrrh were used in the anointing of kings as well as Essene priests, and they were held in gold coffers; these same costly essences were used to anoint the body of the dead, so these "gifts" have tremendous resonance.

The marriage of Joseph and Mary was celebrated for six days by the entire Essene community with feasting and prayer. In addition to many ceremonies of devout prayer and meditation, the Essenes were what would be called great party-givers. They celebrated marriages and births with both solemnity and jollity. Theatrical performances often occupied these rites, along with day-long feasts, ceremonial steam-baths for the men and women of the community, sunrise and sunset group meditations, and general high spirits.

The Gospels inadvertently record many Essene feasts, including the episode of the marriage at Cana, where the first "miracle" of Jesus is recorded. We shall refer to this incident in Chapter Twelve, but for now, suffice it to say that it is a good representation of an Essene wedding, where much wine was consumed.

The picture of early Essene-Christian worship as ascetic is one imposed on the scriptures by later centuries. The Essenes delighted in earthly pleasures, for their philosophy was based on the intermingling of spirit and flesh, not the stoical denial of the bodily pleasures propagated by later revisionists.

The marriage of Joseph and Mary was celebrated by no less than seven hundred participants, all with some connection to the Qumran community. Nearly a hundred different people came each day, joining the ninety regular residents of the community. Each celebrant brought an offering, not to the bride and bridegroom, but to the community, and each was given a small remembrance of this occasion. In the near future some of these tokens, works of exquisite pottery, will be discovered.

This particular marriage was celebrated with unusual ceremony, since the Essenes were aware of its implications. These were the parents of the Essene Messiah, referred to variously in the Essenes' texts as the Great Teacher, the Teacher of Righteousness, and the Host of the Great Spirit.

A distinction must be made regarding the Essenes' belief in this Teacher of Righteousness and the Christ that the historical Jesus has become through the course of history. The Essenes believed that it was possible for any man or woman to become a Teacher of Righteousness, given the proper life-long preparation and training. Their mission, if they indeed had such a cohesive plan for their teaching, was to convince everyone in their world of the possibility of becoming an enlightened being.

This was the goal for each member of their sect, and for any others who crossed the path of the Essenes. They did not hope for a divine one to "descend" to their community, but rather for a great teacher whose life would become an example to others that they, too, could achieve spiritual ascendancy while in human form. In Jesus they received their Great Teacher.

# CHAPTER FOUR

# The Incarnations of Jesus

CHIEF AMONG THE TEACHINGS of the Essenes was the immanence of the invisible world. To the highest members of the sect, the invisible was as present as the physical. After all, their teachings were based on divine revelations to past teachers, such as Buddha, Akhnaton and Moses. "Yahweh", as such, did not speak to the Essenes. In fact, although technically an orthodox Jewish sect, the Essenes did not characterize and personify their god as other Jews did Yahweh.

They believed that avatars, spirits that were by nature angelic forms which had taken fleshly bodies and perfected themselves through many generations and incarnations, were available to those who sought their help, and, when the times so required, these avatars would again take the form of a human and walk among other men. For the avatars, this would be their greatest form of service to mankind; it would also be a reward for having perfected themselves through many incarnations, the reward being one more lifetime than necessary in order to enjoy the pleasures of being in flesh.

In the Essene world-view, each soul was a small piece of divinity that had entered fleshly bodies in order to learn compassion. They believed that each soul had the infinite power of the creator-spirit, and could invent entire worlds and universes, yet, without compassion, that very creative power was of no use except amusement. And compassion could only be learned through duality, yoking pleasure and suffering, the extremes of physical existence.

To the Essenes, Earth was a school, one each soul entered voluntarily for a "crash-course" in compassion. In the course of history, when a society or a people have gone wrong or astray, or forgotten their origin in divinity, an avatar—a great teacher who had gone through many rounds of suffering in earthly lives—could return to flesh and offer one life as an example of the truth of existence.

In the Essene libraries were records of the teachings of many of these avatars, one of which was, as noted before, Akhnaton. Several seers of the Essene community had claimed to receive communications from this spirit that was Akhnaton, and learned, in deep trance states, that this spirit wished to make a final incarnation, as a teaching-tool. Because of Akhnaton's great love for the Jews, that soul would come to troubled Judea, through the bloodline of David.

The message that this avatar-spirit wished to convey was that death, as most mortals understood it, was merely an illusion, a sloughing-off of a mortal body in order to free the spirit. The avatar's life was to end in a dynamic and spectacular way, only to transcend death. In the Akhnaton-Moses Doctrine (see Appendix II), this was one of the greatest lessons each soul came to earth to learn. It was the lesson of the third chakra, the star with six points.

In the Essenes' inner circle there were four couples who were elected to rule the community. One couple were chiefly the administrators of the community's business affairs (Yanuf and Esther at the time of the marriage); one was in charge of the education of the young (these were Miriam's parents); one couple was in charge of the library and "outreach" programs; the fourth couple were seers and healers.

The healing powers of the Essenes were renowned throughout the Middle East, and the "seer" couple performed many of the most miraculous healings. (See Chapter Six on the Essene Mechanics of Healing.) At the time of the birth of Jesus, the couple in charge of this function was a man named Rahab and his wife named Anna beth Sholom (daughter of peace). They predicted the arrival of the avatar spirit, and were to be in charge of the child's spiritual development. They believed that the child of Mary and Joseph would be raised partially by his parents and partially by the Qumran community until his thirty-fifth year, at which time his bodily existence would be filled with the divine spirit.

At the marriage of Mary and Joseph, Rahab and Anna spent a day in counsel with the young couple, advising them of the huge responsibility that would become theirs as soon as Mary conceived, and outlined a plan for the child's spiritual training. At that time, the resources of the Essene community were put at the disposal of the family, and the young couple was assured that their child would want for nothing. In turn, they were asked to raise the child in straitened circumstances, so that, even though both Mary's and Joseph's families were well-to-do, the child was not to be spoiled by luxuries. He was to know how to understand the poorest of the poor as well as the richest of the rich.

Then Rahab and Anna took Mary and Joseph into a smaller chamber, and began to relate the history of the avatar's incarnations. In Essene belief, when a soul re-entered flesh, by the third year of life most memories of prior existences would slowly fade, so that by the end of the seventh year of life, the cycle spent at the first chakra, all past-life memories would have faded. Mary and Joseph were warned, however, that because their child was a great teacher, he would remember his prior incarnations throughout his life, so Rahab and Anna felt it important that the parents be prepared to discuss those incarnations with their child.

In all, they recounted seventy-seven different incarnations stretching back beyond the memories of the races. This spirit was, they told Mary and Joseph, one of the very first soul-entities to enter a fleshly body, and the first eleven incarnations were spent in the task of perfecting the form and shape of the human body. The first spirits to enter flesh entered into imperfect forms, what we refer to today as Cro-Magnons, and their first duties were preparing the human form. The Cro-Magnons had evolved on this planet without a higher consciousness, yet, as most animals do, they yearned for knowledge, the knowledge of good and evil, or, in other words, the meaning behind the duality of earth.

To the Essenes, God was a perfect circle, without opposites or opposition, but this was stasis. The experience of duality, of light and dark, good and evil, life and death held a powerful draw. Earth, as the third planet from the sun, also represented the third chakra or level of energy in a soul's development, and it was this third planet that was, in essence, an experiment with atomic form, specifically carbon, hydrogen and oxygen, which bond in many ways represents a kind of atomic trinity. On this carbon-based planet, creatures of all kinds flourished in order to consume and be consumed.

Angelic souls were never meant to enter this "laboratory", yet the pleasures of consumption and generation drew certain curious souls to this world. The desire to experience this experiment in matter is the symbolic "fall from grace"—that is, the entrance of beings whose existence was entirely without physical matter into bodily forms. Before these spirits entered bodies, they had no knowledge of opposites, only unity. Entering forms on Earth gave them the knowledge of duality, symbolized in many cultures by the "Tree of the Knowledge of Good and Evil".

What these souls also experienced was the kundalini, the sexual energy of all earthly beings, symbolized, as noted above, by the coiled serpent. By entering the bodies of the Cro-Magnons, these first "angelic" spirits were able to experience desire, sexuality, hunger, and death. What they did not bargain for was the powerful draw of duality that obscured the prior memories of unity, of divine perfection.

The Akhnaton avatar, being among the first to enter flesh, spent many lifetimes trying to atone for the process of forgetfulness. Roughly thirty-five lifetimes were spent in forgetting its divine origins, another thirty-five spent in re-awakening that awareness of perfection, and seven spent in teaching. That cycle of seventy-seven, according to Essene belief, had freed that soul from matter forever. Therefore, it was out of love for humanity that this avatar was willing to accept one more life in order to teach a great lesson.

Many of the soul's incarnations were, as mentioned before, engaged in the development and perfection of the human form, as spirit acting upon matter through matter. Many documents in the Essene library outlined how this process, which we call evolution, was brought about in prehistory. The perfection of the human form was a "project" entered into by a great multitude of angelic beings, until the form of mankind as we know it today, in all its various appearances, was perfected. These early "incarnators", in later lives, were possessed of many powers of healing since they, in effect, were the creators and designers of the human body.

Anna and Rahab then told Joseph and Mary of their son's incarnations in many ancient cultures, now lost to history, though mythology remembers them as such nations as Atlantis and Mu, where this newly-created man forgot its origins and became enraptured of its own ego, resulting in a world-wide cataclysm. These early civilizations used both scientific and spiritual power, specifically the power of the atomic trinity, the carbon-hydrogen-oxygen bonds, for the advancement of their own arrogant power, and, after many wars, destroyed the very world they played for. This was, in many ways, the darkest period of human existence, and has been forgotten by mankind for very good reasons.

At the time Jesus was born, there was an intense apocalyptic mood in Judea. The lands of Palestine had suffered under Roman domination, and many revolts arose to rid the land of the conquering troops sent from Rome. A number of Roman governors came and went, yet no one was able to maintain peace. Many Jews believed that the "Last Times" had come, that the world would come to an end. The soul of Jesus, having been present at the "beginning of time", i.e., the temporal existence of angelic beings in bodies of matter, knew better. Through his seventy-seven incarnations, he had learned both the follies and the achievements of mankind only too well to believe that the end of the world was at hand.

Many ancient civilizations perished at their own hands when the "Atlantean" continent was destroyed. The cultures that occupied these lands had unbalanced their environments through unconscionable scientific experimentation, causing the polar ice caps to dissolve and the low-lying lands to be flooded with water. Yet a number of pockets of these civilizations survived, and carried with them remnants of the spiritual learning achieved simultaneously with the technological achievements.

Almost every culture retains a dim racial memory of this cataclysm in its flood-myths; some strange monuments also exist in remote places of these times. What was carried with the remnants of these cultures was also the memory of great teachers, who helped to deliver small pockets of people when the destruction came. Jesus had been one of these teachers, and, after the floods, he returned in a number of incarnations, such as that of Akhnaton, where he tried to influence many cultures which were going astray.

Often this great spirit was not a primary teacher, but one of a school of teachers, subordinate to other masters. Through these "apprenticeships", he learned humility and service to others. This is not to say that the Jesus-spirit was sinless. These many positive lifetimes were spent atoning for selfish and futile lives spent in earlier fleshly entanglements. Through this round of lives, spent over countless centuries, this spirit was one of the first to achieve perfection, a true balance.

It is not of any use to try to outline all of these lives, for many of them were spent in relative obscurity, though several were remembered in legend: Joseph of the Old Testament; Akhnaton, of course; Hammurabi, also in Egypt; Lao Tzu in China; and the Aztec prophet remembered in mythology as Quetzlcoatl, though, surprisingly, the original incarnation that gave rise to the myth was female.

The result of this round of earthly lives was a deep understanding of every human yearning and emotion, and an overwhelming love for all humanity; for Jesus recognized a primary spiritual truth: that every human being is a piece of the endless divinity, dwelling in ignorance of its divine origin and unaware of its unbounded power to create realities.

The final incarnation of this great teacher-soul was to be what became known in Essene teaching as the Loving Demonstration: a clear example to all humanity of the potential all earthly beings share, and the illusion created by the belief in death as a finality. In order to demonstrate the power of the spirit, this final incarnation was to be killed and then rise from the dead.

# CHAPTER FIVE

# The Earthly Life of Jesus

Y'SHUA WAS BORN, as stated, in 4 B.C.E., at the time of the death of the king of Judea, Herod the Great. Although the Gospels relate the story of the Magi and Herod, by which Herod was prompted to kill all the male babies of Bethlehem, this tale is one adopted by later Gospel writers to increase the mythological weight of the Jesus-legend. (Such a massacre could hardly have gone unrecorded by history.) Part Two of this book will outline how later "historians" and "biographers" translated the life of Y'shua into the legend of Jesus Christ.

Here are the facts. He was born in his father's house in Jerusalem, in the spring. The birth was attended by Anna, the seer of the Essenes, and the community's chief healer, a woman named Rachel. Both were trained midwives, and were also seers. They confirmed that at birth, the Great Teacher spirit was, indeed, to inhabit the body of Miriam's child, and, when the child was delivered, they "saw" with their inner sight the glow of enlightenment about the infant's body. In fact, many later images of the

Christ-child showing a "halo" about the baby's head are commemorative of the visions of these two priestesses.

Although this birth was cause for rejoicing among the inner circle of Essenes, it was thought best to keep the identity of the child a secret until he had grown to manhood and claimed his place as a great teacher. Rahab and Anna knew of the mission of this child, and prayed to know at what time he would commence the Great Teaching. Try though they might, they could not divine that time, for once the spirit had entered the frail body of Miriam's child, the seers of the Essenes could no longer communicate with the spirit on a visionary level. It was going to be up to the child himself to determine his own path.

Many so-called "Lost Books of the Bible" purport to tell of the early childhood years of Jesus, but these are for the most part fanciful forgeries of the Fourth Century C.E. and later. In fact, the years of Jesus's infancy were perfectly ordinary and without any miraculous events. As the Essenes were forced to learn, they had to wait for this child to grow to manhood before their "Messiah" would make himself known.

The infant was circumcised according to Jewish law, and raised as a devout Jew of the times. It would be delightfully romantic to say that the child was exquisitely formed, radiantly beautiful, and that his divinity was apparent to all beholders, but in fact the child was perfectly ordinary-looking and seeming. This was, of course, part of the plan of Jesus as a teacher of righteousness. If he appeared to be any different from all other Jews, his point would be lost. He was to be as ordinary as any other Jew, so that every Jew (and gentile, too, for that matter) could look to him and say, "Well, he's just an ordinary man, nothing special about him, and look what he can do! Just imagine what I could do if I follow his advice!"

As soon as the child began to talk, however, he showed a greater-than-average curiosity. The child Jesus seemed to delight in being alive, and no pleasure escaped him. His arrival into the world was followed by several other children of Miriam and Yusef, the next of which was Jacob, better known as James of the New Testament; then his sister Miriam; then his brother Jude or Judas, who looked so much like his elder brother Jesus that he was often called the Twin, which has been translated as Didymus and Thomas, both of which mean "twin"; and then the beloved little sister Ruth.

With such a large family to raise, Miriam was seldom able to keep up with her eldest child's curiosity, and this is where the Essenes entered the picture. Young Y'shua was brought by the gentle Anna to Qumran as soon as he was able to speak, and he was taught many languages in the Essene school. When he learned to read and write these many languages, he began to pore over the many manuscripts in the library, some of which were copies of the very documents brought by Moses from Egypt.

An incident recorded in several journals kept by the Essenes' administrators (written in a curious code) recalls that the child, while reading a papyrus, put the scroll down and began to recite the contents of the document out loud to Rahab and Anna. When they asked him how he had learned what the scroll said, he replied, "I wrote it."

Great pains were taken to keep this prodigious child in line with the development of his fellow children, so that he would retain a kinship with his peers throughout his life. Jesus was encouraged to play and learn with his schoolmates more than half of the day, while the other half was spent in a special course of teaching. The other children were taught in the regular community school by the maternal grandparents of Jesus, while Jesus was tutored privately by Rahab and Anna.

What Rahab and Anna did not count upon, however, was the fact that the child would go home at night and relate whatever he had learned to his siblings. They had intended his training to be for him alone, given their knowledge of the special nature of this soul. Jesus, nonetheless, told his brother James everything. Rahab and Anna spoke to Yusef and Miriam about this, and the child entered the room. Jesus told his aged teachers that he was preparing James to carry on his teachings, and that James should be allowed to be schooled with him.

From that point on, James attended all of the classes with his elder brother, and the two boys, while learning attentively, teased each other and tried to make one another laugh while Rahab and Anna taught them. Although Rahab and Anna took all of their educational processes seriously, James and Jesus, by example, reminded them to always keep a sense of humor and delight in their teachings.

Although the Gospels do not preserve much of what was one of the chief characteristics of Jesus (since none of the four Gospels was written by anyone who actually knew Jesus), even from this early age he was known for his humor. There were few situations which he could not turn into an excuse for laughter. Even as a boy, he knew that in order to be an effective teacher, one must use humor to point up a lesson. Many of the parables of Jesus, as recorded, were more nearly jokes when originally told, causing gales of uproarious laughter.

This does not mean that Jesus should be regarded as a humorist, but he knew that if he made his listeners laugh, they would remember and repeat his stories over and over again. His humor was never malicious, or ever at the expense of any person in particular, but was based on universal human follies and weaknesses. He never exhibited anything but kindness and sympathy for each individual's woes, yet his stories were always full of a rich, earthy humor.

This may come as a surprise to many accustomed to a notion of Jesus as a stern, dour, humorless demi-god. Yet, as a child, he found nothing but delight in humanity, and spent many of his waking hours trying to spread this joy. He was all too well aware of the misery of his countrymen. His father and mother, being well-connected, held many dinners at their home at which the affairs of the day were discussed, and Yusef and Miriam always included their children in these discussions.

Yet Jesus always was able to cut right to the essence of a problem, analyze its cause, cite a reference in the holy books he had studied, and create a piercing but humorous anecdote out of the circumstances of any problem. Many were deeply impressed with the child's powers of mind, and at a very young age, he was invited by the leaders of the Essene community to participate in what could best be termed panel discussions on various topics.

This inclusion in Essene seminars at the age of twelve has passed into the Gospels as the incident where the young Jesus is lost by his parents and found teaching in the Temple. On its face, this story is absurd: how would the "Virgin Mary", knowing her child was of divine birth, lose sight of such a precious boy, forget him in a big city, and then find him lecturing to rabbis? If we pierce the surface of this story, though, we can see how Miriam entrusted her son to the Essene school, "losing" him in a metaphorical way, and "found" him in the "inner sanctum" of the community's forum.

By the age of fourteen, Jesus had absorbed all he could from the Essene libraries, and it was determined that he should be sent to various places around the known world where there were still ancient mystery schools. The Essenes were only one of many such schools, teaching the "secrets" of ancient religions and wisdom. The Qumran community realized that all teachings were basically the same "curriculum" with different terms, images and symbols, and while they imparted all of their collective knowledge to the young Jesus, it was felt that he should experience many different cultures and teachers first-hand.

The so-called Synoptic Gospels record that the Holy Family took the young Jesus to Egypt; although the reason given was to escape Herod's massacre of the innocent babes, since that brutal event did not happen, there must be another reason. In Alexandria, where the great library once stood, there was still a school that taught the ancient initiation rites of Egypt, and Rahab and Anna felt that Jesus should be taken there. And so, in the company of his mother and father, he went.

The other children were taken to the Qumran community house for the duration of the trip, while Jesus, Miriam and Yusef traveled to Alexandria. Rahab and Anna were soon to retire from the community, both being of advanced years, so before the family went on this journey, a feast was celebrated to honor these noble teachers and seers.

Jesus and his family were prepared for in Alexandria, since the Essenes had communicated their arrival to their associates at the mystery school, yet no mention was made of the true nature of the fourteen-year-old boy. It was only made clear that this was a very bright boy, who was to be initiated into the mysteries of Isis and Osiris rather than undergo the Jewish rites of manhood.

Rahab and Anna knew that at the age of fourteen, Jesus would enter another phase of his life, the third cycle. In order to understand this, we should examine some of the healing secrets of the Essenes.

# CHAPTER SIX

# Essene Healing

THE ESSENES' "SECRETS" OF HEALING were not secrets at all, but the result of much study, research, intuitive knowledge and clairvoyant perceptions. As we have noted, great faith was put in the visions, clairvoyant and clairaudient, of the seers of the community, and much Essene training was based on the opening of the "third eye", the eye of inner seeing.

Almost every ancient culture's healing, from India to pre-Columbian America, is based on the same principles. Perhaps the most commonly accepted images were schematized in India, so we will use those terms, but the reader should note that every culture finds its own way to express these same universal truths.

The human body, in esoteric thought, is believed to be made of many other bodies. Some cultures have different numbers, but the Essenes believed in three: the physical, the mental, and the spiritual. They believed that the body, the mind, and the spirit or soul were all interconnected and interpenetrated, and this was yet another manifestation of the divine mystery of the trinity, or tri-unity.

The body consists, then, of three levels, each with its own individual identity but operating together. The most obvious is, of course, the physical, yet according to Essene belief, this body was created—literally brought into being—by the mental body, what we shall call the psychological body.

The simplest way to state this principle was one of the favorite maxims of Jesus: "As you think, so you are." The mind creates the body. The mind, the psychological body, is in turn generated by the spiritual body, sometimes called the "etheric" body. It is at this level that true creativity is known.

The Essenes cherished the idea of God, the Divine Intelligence, as pure creativity. For them, the ultimate mystery was the manifestation of spirit into mind into matter. The critical belief of Essene healing was that if the body was manifesting illness, it was merely a sign or symbol that the mind was ill at ease, or dis-eased. So while the Essene healers could treat the bodily symptoms with herbs and medicines, of which they knew much, they would always probe the mind of each person for the nature of illness.

If the person's mind was deeply troubled, then the Essenes looked to the spirit. Many members of the community were well trained in treatment of the body, like our medical practitioners; others were intuitively gifted in perceiving dis-eases of the mind, like psychologists; but if the problem was on a deeper level, the clairvoyants like Rahab and Anna were called in to trace the problem on the level of spirit.

While the ills of the body were rooted in time, the problems of the mind were less tied to causality, and the disruptions of the spirit were beyond time, the result of karma. Essene healers were able to visualize prior incarnations of each patient, and determine whether or not an illness was of a temporal, psychological or timeless, spiritual cause.

If the cause of an illness was spiritual, the most gifted seers were able to merge with the patients' spirits, trace the cause to a prior incarnation, and, guided by their own inner divinity, either help the patient effect a transformation to erase the karma or accept that no change in the current conditions could be possible... that the patient must endure the karma created in that prior incarnation. But what is karma?

For many, this concept will be familiar; for others, this will be an introduction to a new idea. The word karma means action; in a larger sense, one's karma is the cumulative effect, on a spiritual level, of the actions committed in prior incarnations. To put the idea most simply: a good deed done in one incarnation is manifested as a reward in a future life; a selfish or thoughtless action or deed must be paid back in another life. We hesitate to term anything "evil", since all deeds are repaid in kind.

Again, Jesus was able to put this concept so clearly that all persons could understand it: "As you sow, so shall you reap." What you do to others will come back to you. The Chinese proverb is "plant melons, get melons".

Suppose a life, surrounded by poverty and deprivation, is spent in cheerful service to one's fellow sufferers; those actions are paid in kind by another life in which one is treated kindly. Then suppose the same life in the same circumstances is spent cheating one's fellows out of what little they possess. Those selfish actions will result in another life of abject deprivation.

Yet, as Jesus would remind us, "As you sow, so shall you reap" does not refer to prior or future lives; the effect of one's actions can be felt at once, or perhaps in the near future. If you treat your fellow beings with respect, you will be treated with respect. Treat your brothers and sisters with contempt, and you will be treated that way in return.

Again, Jesus was able to clarify this with economy and elegant clarity: "Do unto others as you would have them do unto you." This is not abstract philosophy, but universal law.

Hence, if the Essene seers perceived that the root of a patient's problem was the result of actions in a prior existence, an intuitive assessment was made as to whether or not that patient had learned a lesson from that experience. If so, then a healing could take place. If not, the patient was advised that it was a direct result of earlier karma, and the patient was then counseled as to a course of action to take by which they could become aware of their misdeeds and rectify them through service to mankind and God.

What the Essene healers stressed was twofold: first, they did not perform the healings, but rather let the God-power of the universe work through them; secondly, they could not allow a healing to take place if the soul of the patient did not will it so. Perhaps this will be clear if we look at a famous example.

There is an incident in the Gospels were Jesus is approached by a blind woman, who asks to be healed. The disciples of Jesus ask him, "Who sinned that this woman was born blind, she or her parents?" (The woman, incidentally, was changed to a man by the Gospel writers for reasons we shall examine later.) Jesus looks at the blind beggar, and replies, "Neither. She was born blind so that the glory of God could be made manifest through her." And the woman is healed of her blindness.

Even though all references to reincarnation were apparently excised from the Gospels, this story could not be taken out, yet cannot be explained without reference to reincarnation. How, otherwise, could this woman be born blind unless she sinned in a prior life?

Jesus was able to see into the woman's prior incarnation where the blindness was caused, and determine that the woman, in her present life, had learned her lesson. He could also determine that she had atoned enough for whatever she had done to ask forgiveness of her spirit. Acting as a guide, he helped her ask her soul—her indwelling God—for forgiveness, and the woman was healed not by the "person" of Jesus but by the divinity the two shared on the deepest level of existence, and all in an instant, since this forgiveness existed outside of earthly time.

Yet in another case, Jesus was unable to manifest a healing since the patient who sought to be healed was not ready to forgive himself, and wanted Jesus to "repair" him. Jesus saw, as all Essene healers could, that the karma had not been repaid, that a lesson had not been learned.

As his Essene teachers had shown Jesus, all healing happened on the level of the soul, the level of the divine. Merely "fixing" the body does not change the awareness of the patient's mind and spirit. The blind woman was ready for the "miracle" of sight, for she was aware of her karma and also of her own divinity, so the blindness was no longer necessary as a teaching-tool.

This is the only "secret" of Essene healing, that the body is a teaching-tool for the mind, and the mind is a teaching-tool for the spirit. A "miracle" of healing is merely the three bodies, the mental, the physical, and the spiritual, working in accordance with divine law, the laws of the universal divinity.

To elaborate about the three bodies, the interpenetration of the mental, physical and spiritual happens at seven centers in the being, the seven chakras mentioned earlier. Medicine has shown us that at those seven centers, there are the so-called "ductless" glands in the physical body, about which much is known, but the actual operation of these glands is still much of a mystery to those who see the body only in physical terms.

Yet by imagining the other two bodies superimposed upon the physical, the seven centers in the mental and spiritual bodies correspond to those ductless glands, and it is at those points that the subtler energies of mind and spirit merge. We have also mentioned the kundalini, the dynamic energy of the body, which is often thought of as a coiled serpent when it lies dormant in the pelvis.

Ancient mystery-school teaching shows us that each chakra is filled with a vortex of spiritual, mental and physical energy every seven years. At birth, the bottom chakra or wheel of energy is filled, and the kundalini should move up every seven years thereafter. At seven years, the age at which formal schooling usually begins, the second wheel is inundated with energy. Another major change occurs at fourteen, then at twenty-one, at twenty-eight, thirty-five, and so on.

These energies move up in three channels. One corresponds to the spine; the others weave in and out from side to side, threading through each chakra. When this diagram is abstracted from the body (see illustration), you will recognize the Caduceus of Mercury used by, among others, the American Medical Association.

## THE CADUCEUS

We have seen that at fourteen, when the energies moved through the second wheel toward the third, Jesus was taken to Egypt for his initiation into manhood.

# CHAPTER SEVEN

# Jesus in Egypt

W HEN HE WAS TAKEN to Egypt, the young Jesus was shocked to find that the land was familiar to him. The very sight of the plains near Alexandria and, most especially, the later approach to the pyramids filled his mind with visions of previous lives spent in those places. Before he could be told of his purpose in the journey, he "knew" by his inner sight what it was that he was to learn in Egypt. He told his parents that he was to experience a death and entombment ritual as part of his mystery initiation, and that in this ritual he would discover the true mission of his life.

While much of his training and preparation at the Qumran school had given him the background for this flash of enlightenment, Jesus was not aware of his life's purpose on an experiential level until this moment. It was precisely at this moment that the aged Anna, back at Qumran, passed from her earthly life. She had prepared this exceptional child well, and left earthly existence knowing that her work was to be continued by other hands. She is memorialized, although disguised, in the extant

Gospel of Luke as a "great and venerable prophetess".

The family was welcomed by the leader of the mystery school in Alexandria, which was housed in a simple, earth-floored dwelling. At that time, much so-called "mystery" teaching was conducted in secret, for it contradicted "state" religions. Even though the Romans occupied Judea, they allowed the Jews to maintain their beliefs, since any attempt to "convert" the Jews to the Roman pantheon of gods would create war. In other Roman provinces, however, the occupying armies were less tolerant of other native religions, and persecuted those who did not succumb to the Roman modes of thinking. This was the case in Roman-occupied Egypt.

As a result, this famous mystery school was headquartered in a modest hut, tended by a few aged priests. There was no library, no communal study or debating room, in fact, no guest quarters such as Jesus knew at Qumran. The head of the school, Amnon Abdullah Mukkarah, who was genially called "Amneris" (after the ancient god) by his fellows, sheltered the family in his sister's house, then took the young Jesus into the desert.

Out in the desert, Amneris asked Jesus what existed there to support life. Jesus replied that there was nothing he could see that would support any kind of life, and could see no life. Amneris told him to become still, close his eyes, and begin to sense what was around him. The young boy, entering into a deep state of meditation and relaxation as he had been taught, began to sense movement around him. He "saw" that the sands were full of myriad crawling creatures, thousands of tiny plants, even millions of micro-organisms, all carrying on the endless flow of life. Amneris was pleased by the boy's inner awareness. He told him, "That is the first lesson the desert can teach you. God is everywhere, and even where he seems most absent, he provides for all his creatures. My son, in the middle of this desert, if so many creatures are fed and nurtured by his generosity, you can live anywhere and through anything as long as you trust that God is providing for you."

The two, the old man and the boy, then returned silently to the mystery school. There they sat together in meditation, while Amneris divined the nature of the boy's mission. He asked Jesus if he loved his father and his mother. Jesus replied that he did, citing the Mosaic commandment that required him to do so. Amneris told him, "You have no mother and father, boy, except God. The people who gave you form did not create you.

You are in their care, but your mother and your father is God. God is male and female, dark and light, all things in all things. All things come from God and return there. Do you understand?"

Jesus replied, "If I have no father and no mother except God, then every man is my brother. Is that right?" Amneris was very pleased with the boy's insight. "It is obvious you have no need of my teaching," Amneris said, "for it seems you can teach me many things. Why have you come to me?"

Jesus answered, "I have come to know death." "Many men fear death," Amneris said. "Do you, wise boy?" Jesus replied, "Since I have known death many times in many lives and have come back to live in this world, I have no reason to fear death. But I must know about death."

Amneris recognized these words as the beginning of the most sacred initiation rites of the ancient Egyptian mysteries as introduced by Amen-Ho-Tep, the scribe of Akhnaton. Amneris left and found the parents of Jesus.

"He is very wise," Amneris told Miriam and Yusef, "so wise that he need not spend any time in training. I must take him to the pyramids at once." Miriam and Yusef agreed to let Amneris take their son on the long journey. Along the way, Jesus and Amneris spent many hours conversing about ideas and questions the boy had. Amneris was able to inform Jesus of the Egyptian teachings and beliefs relating to each of his questions, yet was always surprised at the insight Jesus brought to each issue.

Finally, at the great pyramid, the two were met by a party of nine. Jesus was surprised to find these people there. Amneris told Jesus that he had been in communication with these nine on a super-conscious level, "calling" them to the site. Here this party of nine, all adepts at mystery training, were to initiate Jesus into the secrets of their traditions.

At night, the nine seers built a great fire in the desert. They sat around the fire in a circle and chanted. Jesus and Amneris stood outside this circle, walking around and around. Finally, Amneris asked to be admitted to the circle. The leader of the nine asked, "Who is to be admitted?" "Y'shua, a wise young man." "Who is his father?" was the next question. Amneris said, "He has no father but God." "Who is his mother?" "He has no mother but God," came the second reply. The leader of the nine then looked directly at Jesus. "Why were you born?" Jesus trembled and said, "I do not know."

Then the circle began a song, an ancient song of Osiris:

*"As Osiris the mighty fell from the sky to the earth,*
*The clay of the earth received his foot.*
*He walked upon the earth for many years, yet knew not why.*
*He asked the earth, but the earth answered him not.*
*Osiris prayed to know, and the earth opened and received him.*
*Osiris went into the earth, to the land of the dead.*
*There he learned why he was born.*
*Osiris returned from the land of the dead.*
*The earth opened, and he knew many things.*
*He was born to die, and live again, and fear not death."*

The nine took Jesus, removed his robe, and laid him upon a linen sheet they had put upon the sand. With many prayers and supplications, they anointed his body with embalming spices, then wrapped his body in the linen sheet. Jesus was frozen with fear. The nine lifted his body and carried it into the great pyramid. They went through chamber after chamber, and Jesus could not see where he was being taken. Finally, they reached the innermost chamber of the pyramid, and placed Jesus into a stone sarcophagus. They intoned prayers of the dead over him, then left, moving a great stone over the opening to the chamber. Jesus, fatigued by the long days of travel, hungry from fasting and dazed from the near-hallucinogenic aromas of the embalming spices, entered into a deep dream state, where he first heard the voice of Amneris saying, "Where God seems most absent, he is there and everywhere."

Jesus felt only the cold stone and heard only the total silence of the tomb, then heard another voice that repeated over and over the words "I AM". Jesus followed that voice into the deepest reaches of his being, repeating "I AM" until he felt that he was going to shudder his body into pieces. He had gone far beyond fearing the cold quiet of death, for the voice lifted his mind and soul into a realm of pure existence, one without end. He felt his body shake, shudder, and tremble as if it were coming apart, and then, in a blinding flash, he found himself standing in an outer chamber, surrounded by Amneris and the nine. Jesus was unclad, and Amneris came to him with a loose linen robe.

Amneris told Jesus, "He whom we left for dead is risen. You are reborn.

Osiris was in the land of the dead for three days. For three days you have lain in the tomb. Can you remember anything of that time?" Jesus said, "I am hungry." Amneris and the nine whooped with joy and laughter, and brought forth baskets of food for the boy, who ate voraciously. The solemn mood was broken. The leader of the nine said to Jesus, "Often we have to break in and take the young men out, they cry so much and so soon. Never have we waited so patiently and then been so surprised." "Why are you surprised?" Jesus asked. "Look behind you," the leader answered. The stone that sealed the tomb chamber had not been moved.

The next morning, Jesus met again with Amneris and the nine. After a night's sleep, Jesus wanted to know what had happened. He was told that the nine had kept a vigil outside the tomb chamber, staying clairvoyantly in tune with the boy in case he should panic. The initiation ceremony was to teach the initiate that death was imaginary, and that the "I AM" of God, the eternal existence of spiritual life, transcends death. Jesus remarked that while he had studied that idea, he never felt it until he was in the tomb. "That is the mystery of death," Amneris told him. "You feel God in every part of your being, and can do anything, even pass through the stone walls of the tomb."

After this, Amneris took Jesus back to Alexandria and returned him to his parents. Amneris warned Miriam and Yusef not to question the boy about his initiation, merely to listen if he wanted to talk to them about it. "Do not be amazed if he is much changed," Amneris told them, "for he has learned that you are not his parents. From now on, he is a Son of God." Because of their own schooling at Qumran, Miriam and Yusef understood what the old Egyptian meant, and prepared to take Jesus back home. They asked Amneris if they were to have any scrolls or books to take, and Amneris replied, "Now Jesus will know all things directly from their Source. Anything he wants to know, the Spirit of God will come and tell him."

# CHAPTER EIGHT

# Travels of Jesus

THIS INITIATION RITE HAS many forms in ancient cultures. While it is almost always performed at the time a young man passes into manhood, roughly at fourteen years of age, it is also part of the initiation of young girls into womanhood. In Native American cultures the form is different, and it is called a "Vision Quest", but it always provokes a profound change in the life of the initiate.

The Jesus who returned to Judea with Miriam and Yusef was indeed changed. While the bright boy with the sunny disposition they had raised still shone through, Jesus now spent many hours in silence, his brow furrowed. He often refused to talk for days, to his parents' dismay. They were afraid the boy was becoming too moody and depressed. Miriam went to her brother Joseph of Arimithea, who was a rich merchant, but was also familiar with many different schools of religion. (For purposes of clarity, we shall refer to Joseph of Arimithea as "Joseph" and the father of Jesus as "Yusef"). Joseph of Arimithea, it may be remembered, had endowed the library at Qumran with many volumes he had collected and was, in fact, the chief patron of the community.

Joseph of Arimithea questioned his nephew and found that the young man was not at all withdrawn, but so deeply disturbed by the suffering he saw around him that he could not speak. "Why don't all men know what I know, that God provides for all needs? Why are men so unhappy?" Joseph told Jesus that the people of Judea were unhappy because of the Romans. "But don't the Romans also know what I learned in Egypt? Why are people so concerned with worldly problems that they don't see the true reality of the world?" Joseph confessed that he had no answers, but told Jesus that he was about to embark on a series of voyages to several different countries, and asked Jesus if he wanted to accompany him. "You'll see how people in other lands have answered some of the same questions." Jesus agreed to go with his uncle, and Miriam and Yusef were grateful that their son was so interested in the voyage.

Miriam, as she was packing Jesus's clothes, expressed concern about the boy's safety on such a long sea voyage, but Jesus replied, "I know now that God is my father and my mother, as he is yours. If you do not trust in my safety, you do not trust God." Shamed, Miriam kissed her boy and gave him his bundle. Jacob, (hereinafter "James"), the second son of Miriam and Yusef, wanted to go on the trip as well, and Jesus persuaded his parents to allow James to go along. Jesus had not spoken of his mystical experience in Egypt to any of his brothers or sisters, but he promised James that he would relate it at length once they had set sail.

The first leg of the journey of Joseph the Merchant was to go to the south of Gaul, which is now France. Joseph's crew was to trade there for fine wools, spices, wine, dried fruits and grains, then proceed on to the Roman encampments in Britain. Joseph had many friends in Gaul, where he and his nephews and the ship's crew were lavishly entertained, but he did not stay long. Joseph had planned his journey so that Jesus could spend time at another famous mystery school in Britain.

Of the many cultures with which Joseph of Arimithea was familiar, he had the strongest ties to a remnant of a Celtic sect in the west of what is now England, in the town known today as Glastonbury. Even to this day, many legends about Joseph and Jesus persist there, and some readers may be familiar with William Blake's poem "Jerusalem", which suggests that Jesus did visit Britain.

Joseph of Arimithea actually had little commerce with this village, but used his voyages as an excuse to travel there. He introduced Jesus and James to another mystery school there, and enrolled them in a month's study. This was a mystery school of a different order, for in Glastonbury the training Jesus received had more to do with learning of the many properties of plants and the nature kingdom. In the rugged, stormy seaport town (which is today a fair distance from the sea), he was told of the many forces of nature, of non-physical entities that shape the natural world; these forces have been called in folklore and legends elves, fairies and elementals, but, as Jesus was taught, they are members of the angelic realms that do not take human form but rather shape the non-human physical world.

Through this intense training, the boys learned why and how plants have medicinal powers (which was taught but not fully understood at Qumran, even though the healing school there was legendary) and learned that all living things have spirits and are, like humans, manifestations of God. Particular to this school was a strong belief that the earth itself is a living, sentient being obeying universal law. Just as his entombment initiation in Egypt had shown Jesus his true nature, here he learned of his physical and spiritual connection to all forms of life on earth. The bridge between all forms, he was taught, is the force of God-energy.

While in Britain, Jesus learned of other cultures and other beliefs, yet he also saw the same Roman domination that he had known in his native land and in Egypt. This troubled the sensitive boy no end, and he, James, and their uncle spent many nights on board Joseph's trading vessel wrestling with the problem of misery, oppression and suffering.

"Many men try to rise against their oppressors in war-like ways," Joseph said. "Without a doubt, this leads to a loss of life on a horrible scale. War only seems to breed more war." Jesus asked, "Why should brother fight against brother?" James chimed in, saying that he and his brothers often disagreed, and had sometimes fought. "But did that settle anything?" Joseph asked. James said that it only made his brothers resentful, bent on vengeance. Jesus remembered his studies in Mosaic law, which said, "Vengeance is God's."

Joseph reminded the boys that this did not mean that God is vengeful, but that men should not attempt to balance the scales of justice through vengeful acts. "Those who live by violence are sure to die by violence. That is universal law. Those who live peacefully and know God may also die in violence," Joseph said. "Why is that?" James asked. Jesus answered, speaking for the first time about what he had learned in Egypt, "Men do not know that death is an illusion, and think that they can use death to conquer others. But the law of karma brings death upon the conquerors, while those unjustly punished shall return to a life of reward. If all men knew that death is an illusion, and that all men are brothers, they would know that every man who oppresses another only oppresses himself and his brother."

"If only all men could learn that, there would not be so much needless suffering," said Joseph. Jesus grew pale. James asked him what was wrong. "That is the lesson I have come to teach," said Jesus. "In time I shall know how I shall reveal it to my brothers, but I know now what I must say."

In a flash, Jesus had realized that his mission on earth was twofold: he was to tell all men that they are brothers; and he was to likewise tell them that death is an illusion, that life is neverending and eternal. There, on board Joseph's ship, he realized that the only way to make those points was not through writing, for few could read, or preaching, for few could understand such ideas on an abstract level, but through illustration.

In order to demonstrate that all people are connected by a common bond, that all men are manifestations of divine energy and compassion, Jesus knew that he must be able to show that the boundaries of flesh are illusory, and this demanded miracles. In order to make people re-think their self-imposed limitations, a miracle shatters those boundaries and opens the eyes of the recipient to the infinite possibilities of the Divine.

Yet Jesus knew that if he was indeed to manifest such miracles, he was still unprepared. In consulting with his uncle Joseph on the ship, it was determined that Jesus should continue his studies with other teachers in other lands, so that he might more clearly understand how to overcome the boundaries of the flesh and the world. Jesus had had one manifestation of such a miracle in the pyramid-tomb, when he passed bodily through a stone barrier. That very action had shown to Jesus the power of the Divine inside him, and had proven the fact that death was merely an illusion, that the soul-energy of his being could exist apart from, and transcend, the frail limitations of his body.

Plans were drawn up for the further travels and studies of Jesus. Joseph of Arimithea had many friends in distant lands, and he could arrange for Jesus to study first in Persia with a school of mystics who manifested Divine Law; and then Jesus would study with spiritual adepts in India who would teach him how to transcend the limits of the body.

The goal of Jesus was clear: he was to learn and experience all of these teachings, assimilate them, and return to his beloved Jews living under Roman domination, and become their Messiah, their liberator. The Jews of Palestine were expecting a Messiah who would lead a revolt against Rome, but what Jesus knew he must bring back to Judea was the only true way to escape oppression: the liberation of the soul into the Divine Love of God. Through this struggle, he would be able to show his people that their suffering under the Roman forces could be transcended not from without, but from within.

# CHAPTER NINE

# Travels in the Near and Far East

BEFORE TRACING WHAT JESUS LEARNED in the remainder of his travels, we should digress at this point to clarify certain things. The initiation rite, in which Jesus apparently passed through a wall of stone, was designed to cause the initiate to confront his fear of death, and by spending time in a darkened tomb, overcome that fear and realize that God is present in all things. In the case of Jesus, however, the ceremony went one step further, and awakened all of his past-life memories in which he had experienced a glimpse of the Divine Force. In that second he was able to become pure energy, dissolving his physical body, and just as quickly re-assemble his form.

While this process may seem startling, more unusual than any so-called miracles reported in the Synoptic Gospels, the ancient world and its spiritual adepts understood that form is illusory, and that the mind of man constantly creates the form of the body. In his previous incarnations, Jesus had experienced such knowledge, and had further training at Qumran of those principles. However, he would have been unable to perform such a startling feat without the support of the mystics of the Alexandria School and the particular design of the pyramid, which is not, as is commonly believed, the tomb of an ancient Pharaoh but is the temple of initiation into the Egyptian Mysteries, specifically designed for such purposes. Buried deep under the Great Pyramid is a hall of records, in which many documents containing the collected wisdom of the ancient world's civilizations are stored; this chamber has not yet been discovered, but may perhaps be found within the near future. Stored in this room are documents that outline atomic theories about the mutability of matter and energy that are attributed in our time to Einstein and his followers.

In truth, what Einstein realized, in a dream-like hypnagogic state, was a facet of eternal, cosmic law that had remained hidden until the world was prepared to rediscover it. Such "secrets" of the universe—for example, Einstein's theory of the mutability of matter into energy—reveal how matter is created, and were indeed the basis of ancient so-called "occult" doctrines (for the word "occult" simply means "hidden").

Because of the cataclysms referred to earlier in the ancient world when such theories were made common knowledge (such as the legendary destruction of Atlantis—a highly developed scientific society), it was thought provident to "hide" this knowledge from the common world after such destruction. This information was only to be revealed to those who had proven themselves spiritually pure and altruistic enough not to abuse such precious knowledge, hence the creation of the "Mystery Schools".

What Jesus went to learn in Britain, in Persia, and in India was this very knowledge. In previous lives he had possessed, and indeed, in some cases, helped to codify such knowledge, but in pieces: part of the knowledge in one life, and part in others. What was necessary for him, he realized, was to assemble all the knowledge that he could into one grand doctrine that would have universal meaning. By traveling and studying in all of these cultures, he was able to see that each culture has its own terms of expressing what are universal realities. What held for Jesus in ancient Palestine is true in modern-day America. What changes, however, is vocabulary and nuance. This is why so many of the teachings of Jesus are so often misinterpreted.

In the time of Jesus, roughly 4 B.C.E. to 70 C.E., there was no word for the ego. True it is that the ancient Greeks had actually defined such a concept, the daimon, but it was not until the work of Freud and Jung that the modern concept of the ego and the id were defined. In our culture, we all understand in a general way what these concepts embody. However, in the time and land of Jesus, there was another concept that stood for the same idea, and that was Satan or the Devil. In his education, Jesus was well aware of what the ego was about: the base, selfish part of the psyche that identifies with the body and external form, denying the larger part of the soul.

What's more, those around Jesus understood that this is what he meant when he spoke of the Devil or Satan. It was not until much later than the time of Jesus that this concept of the ego was melded with Eastern and Greco-Roman ideas to create a "fallen angel" persona, a separate being that lived in Hell (Gehenna) and tempted men towards evil. This crude concept of "Satan" as a powerful being at war with an external God-figure in "Heaven" debases the finer points of the teachings of Jesus.

Most references in the existing Gospels to a God in Heaven mean the indwelling Divinity common to all men, just as references to "Satan" or the Devil refer to what we would call the ego. Therefore, when the Gospels say that Jesus went into the wilderness and was tempted by the Devil, the meaning is that Jesus, in isolation, wrestled with his ego. He had learned the mysteries of the universe as revealed in the Mystery School teachings, and was torn, as any man who learns such monumental truths would be: he could use them to his own ends, selfishly, for material gain, oppressing his fellow men; or he could, from a more divine perspective, use these powers and "secrets" to help his brothers.

This is why such teachings have been considered secret through history. As we have seen in our times, when the laws of the universe that can create and destroy matter are used without regard for the common good and spiritual advancement of mankind, they become destructive and, if the word may be so applied, evil. In the Eden myth, this is what is meant by the "Knowledge of Good and Evil", symbolized by the tree. Seen from the perspective of divinity, there is no good and evil, and all men and women are united by their common God-hood. However, when viewed from a perspective of duality, in which good and evil are absolutes and opposing forces, there is only war and struggle.

What Jesus realized in all of his travels was that, no matter what the culture, the principles that created the universe were the same. Joseph of Arimithea, while he traveled widely and was devoted to mystical teaching, knew all of this on a theoretical level, but Jesus was determined to know the great teachings of these many civilizations on an experiential level, having done so in Alexandria.

While in Britain, Jesus and James learned many techniques of healing with plants, and ways of cooperating with nature and the elements. This knowledge supplemented ideas learned in Palestine, and also awakened memories stored in the mind of Jesus. Yet this learning only created a greater hunger. Jesus wanted to know more and more. Joseph was arranging a journey to Persia and the Far East soon after his return from Gaul and Britain, and suggested to Jesus that he go on this voyage.

In the meantime, the boys had returned to Jerusalem. At the time they returned, the Romans had changed Proconsuls, replacing a sensitive but militarily ineffectual governor with a cruel and militant officer, who had served as a commander in several Roman army campaigns and was being "rewarded" with the Judean post. This commander was Gaius Lucius Mutius. During his reign, he barely tolerated the Jewish King and Sanhedrin, and increased the presence in Jerusalem of Roman soldiers and centurions. While the occupying Romans in previous times had co-existed with the Jews, Mutius was going to make Jerusalem a Roman city under Roman rule.

Yusef and Miriam, being well connected with the priests and the Jewish politicians, had decided that, in order to remain both safe and politically neutral, they should move to a house owned by Yusef's family in Capernaum, at the north end of the Sea of Galilee. It is here that the age-old myth of Yusef being a carpenter arose, for while the family did not occupy the house, it had been rented to a carpenter and his family, and became known in Capernaum as "The Carpenter's House". So when Yusef and Miriam moved there with their other children, even though they owned the house, it had become identified with the recently-departed carpenter.

Messianic fervor in Jerusalem grew stronger as the Romans increased their fortifications and occupying presence. More and more Jews were convinced that the "last times" were at hand and cried out for the Messiah to deliver them. While James and Jesus were away on their voyage (which lasted almost a year), there had been several uprisings and as many "Messiahs", all of which had been quashed by the Roman troops. Several priests of the Temple who secretly supported the rebels died mysteriously, and rumors circulated that they had been poisoned by spies of the Proconsul.

Because Miriam and Yusef, as well as the Essene Brotherhood, had believed that Jesus would be the Messiah, they were afraid that the political fervor of the times would push Jesus into assuming that role before he was ready, and feared that the brilliant young man would be seduced by political zealots. (The Zealots were a fierce party of the time who cried loudest and longest for the Messiah to come.) They felt that they should inform him of their plans openly. Jesus agreed with their move, saying, "I know my time has not yet come." What's more, Jesus wished to accompany Joseph on his Far East travels, and the family could not have been happier.

Again, Jesus wanted James to go with him. James, although deeply loved by his brother, was not of the same mystical bent as Jesus. James was delighted with his knowledge learned in Britain, and was eager to see the lands of Persia and India, but was not as keen on the rigorous training in meditation that Joseph told about. Jesus insisted that James go along and take the training. He told James, "When I return, I shall start to teach my brothers and sisters what I have learned. This will take all of my time and energy. You, James, are of a more logical mind, and you must understand what I am doing, and help me organize the people who will follow me. In time, you may become the leader of the movement I will start toward freedom."

James interpreted this in a more political way than Jesus meant it. James thought that his brother would, indeed, lead a revolt against Rome, while Jesus knew that the revolution he intended was one of the spiritual and intellectual side of man. "Don't you know," he said to James, "that as soon as the Romans leave Judea, there will come another, and another, and another to occupy the land? If we Jews cannot maintain peace and harmony among ourselves, how are we ever to resist conquerors? I will lead our people to a place where they are free, and where they have always been free. I plan to lead them to the Kingdom of God."

James replied, "Our forefather Moses was going to lead our people to the Promised Land, and they wandered forty years in the wilderness. Where are you taking us now? Where is this new kingdom?" Jesus looked him deeply in the eyes. "The Kingdom of God is inside you, and inside me, and inside everyone who has ever lived. You are God and I am God, and every one of the Romans is God." James was shocked. "Are you saying that our enemies are our brothers?" Jesus smiled. "Of course. Why, then, should our brothers be our enemies? As much as I love you, my brother, should you and I love the Romans, our enemies." James was distressed. He couldn't imagine how he could ever bring himself to such a position.

"Aren't you yourself angry about what the Romans have done to our land and our people? Many a time I've heard you storm about their injustices," James said to Jesus. "You shouldn't judge people by their actions," Jesus answered. "May I not hate what the Romans have done, yet love and forgive them?"

James thought a moment. "If you are going to be the Messiah, this sort of talk isn't going to make you very popular." Jesus answered, "Maybe I won't be the Messiah. Maybe you will." James was stunned, and Jesus continued, "Each one of us has the potential to become the Messiah, for each of us is equal in the sight of God." James protested, "But the Messiah is going to lead the people of Israel against the Romans." Jesus laughed. "The only way to defeat an enemy is to love him. If you love your enemy, he cannot be your enemy any longer. The Roman ways cannot be stopped until I change the Roman heart, and our resistance against the Romans cannot succeed until I change the hearts of our people from hatred to love."

"And how exactly do you plan to do this?" James asked. Jesus thought a moment. "I don't know, but perhaps you and I can talk about it on our trip." James was puzzled, but intrigued. He did not fully understand what Jesus had in mind, but he was thrilled at the prospect of being a part of it, whatever it might become.

As soon as their family was safely moved to the house in Capernaum, the two brothers and their uncle were about to set sail. Joseph of Arimithea was obliged to give a portion of all of his trade to the Romans as tribute, in addition to the stiff taxes being imposed by Mutius, and as a result was friendly with many of the tax collectors who, while Jews, worked for Rome and were despised by the devout. Joseph sailed under a Roman warrant, which allowed him free passage through blockaded cities, if necessary, and had to keep abreast of political developments. Just before he sailed, he learned that the Romans were about to levy another, even higher tax, and were, therefore, about to conduct a census. As a result, he had to delay his voyage for several months.

During this time, while idle in Capernaum, Jesus traveled all over the neighboring country, trying to get a sense of what the northern people thought. Used to the relative urbanity and sophistication of Jerusalem, Jesus found these country people to be less guileful and more honest. He began to love their bluntness and earthiness. Moreover, he began to appreciate their earthy humor. Many of the people in the north were farmers and shepherds, and were consequently closer to the land than those Jesus knew in the cities. Among these simple people, Jesus demonstrated many of the healing skills he had learned in Qumran and Glastonbury, and developed a small reputation as a healer. During his first months in Capernaum, he cured many illnesses, refusing payment but accepting goods in return. It must be recalled that none of these healings were of the sort reported later as "miracles" in the Gospels, yet by today's medical standards, we would regard some of these cures as miraculous. Yet, because he had seen the results of these processes over and over, Jesus trusted in the ability to heal. He knew that he could never take credit for these cures, as many wonder-workers of Jerusalem did.

In Jerusalem there were many who made their reputations on miraculous cures, and many were quite famous. One, in particular, named Ainah, was the physician to the Court. Yet the Essenes, many of whom practiced the same cures, knew that healing was a process of the indwelling God, and that the physician merely facilitated the body's desire for wholeness. The Essenes denounced Ainah, because he claimed to have "special" and "magical" powers, and traded on such to gain wealth and power. Under Mutius, Ainah found that he could worm his way into Roman favor and, as soon as he did, he persuaded Mutius to discredit the Essenes. Ainah persuaded the Proconsul that the Essenes were practicing "abominations" and fomenting dissent and revolution. Ainah had managed to learn that the Essenes claimed to harbor a Messiah, and, convincing Mutius that they planned to attack (taking the Messiah for a revolutionary), persuaded Mutius to sack the settlement at Qumran.

Fortunately for the Essenes, they had friends in the right places, tax collectors who informed Joseph of Arimithea what was in the wind. Joseph was able to send word to the Qumran community to scatter, and recommended that they secure as many of the manuscripts in their library as possible. The scribes and keepers of the documents at Qumran hid many of the most valuable scrolls in earthen jars in caves, some of which have been found in recent times, and some of which are still hidden. Yet the wise scribes went one step further: they created forged and facetious documents which they left in the library for the Romans to find. Most of the leaders and residents of the community then scattered, and the few that were left willingly turned their "library" over to the Roman troops. As a result, the Romans couldn't find anything incendiary in the documents, and the leaders of the community were all spared.

Nevertheless, Mutius had the buildings razed, and issued a decree prohibiting the Essenes from formal assembly. Because of the political changes in and around Jerusalem, many people became spies for the Romans (Roman spies were secretly exempted from taxation), so the Essene Brotherhood went "underground". This is why there are no references to the Essenes as such in the Gospels, for they formally ceased to exist before the events in the life of Jesus recorded therein. Unfortunately, many of the forged and "decoy" documents persisted. Since these "dummy" documents were both coded and innocuous, they presented a false and insignificant image of the Essenes, and some of these were relied upon by early Gospel writers as Essene tracts.

A word is in order at this moment about the four Gospels. None of the four that are in the New Testament—Matthew, Mark, Luke and John—was written before 64 C.E. None was written by people who knew Jesus personally. Mark was the first to be written, yet it was based on an earlier scroll, which itself drew heavily upon oral tradition and fragments of "decoy" documents that had passed into Roman hands. As a result, the Gospel of Mark incorporates references to Essene thoughts that were erroneous forgeries. Luke was written about a decade later, and was based almost entirely on Mark. Matthew is almost entirely a forgery, assembled from bits and pieces of older manuscripts (including Mark) and circulated by Paul for propaganda purposes. (See Chapter Twenty-One for a full discussion of this.) John's Gospel, while similar to the others, was based on a Greek version, itself a translation of a document used as a source by Mark, but which also relied upon oral traditions handed down by Essene families and, significantly, a book by Jude, Jesus's brother; therefore, John's Gospel is closer to Essene thought than the other three. Suffice it to say at this point that none of the Four Gospels is without additions, revisions, alterations and distortions, and are all, at least in most versions, translations from even later Greek versions.

Because the family of Jesus had moved to Capernaum, and because many documents of the Essenes that the Romans seized were calculatedly misleading, the Romans found no evidence of a "Messiah-in-training" at Qumran. The members of the community were now scattered throughout Judea, and the Essene movement, as it once existed, was for all appearances disbanded.

Yet the members of the Essenes held onto their beliefs, and were in constant communication with one another, although for appearances, their meetings and meditation sessions were made to look like social gatherings. Despite Roman evidence that the Essenes were ascetics (as existed in documents made available to historians like Josephus), this was a myth perpetrated by the scribes when creating their "decoys", so that the Romans would think that the Essenes were apolitical and so that the erroneous claims of Ainah that the Essenes were "lewd and licentious" could be refuted.

Nothing, of course, could have been farther from the truth, yet the myth still persists through history that the Essenes were ascetics, practicing celibacy and abstinence from wine. Paul, having no direct access to Essene thought, learned all he knew about their beliefs through the same Roman-owned forgeries, which he combined with his own personal views to create what is now perceived as early Christian beliefs. (See Chapter Nineteen for more information about Paul's personality and distortions of historical truth.)

Even though Ainah and Mutius could find no harm in the Essenes, Ainah was convinced that the sect would send a fiery leader against Rome, and was tireless in his quest to find the "Messiah". Mutius called the case closed once the Qumran community buildings were destroyed, but Ainah enlisted the aid of Herod Antipas, son of Herod the Great, who was the impotent but titular King of the Jews, and ruler of the northern province of Galilee. Ainah convinced Herod Antipas (hereafter, simply "Herod") that the Essene Messiah was trying to raise an army against him and the Romans, and so Herod became ferocious in his prosecution of any who claimed to lead a revolution.

In light of all of this uproar, Jesus ceased his ministrations among the Galileans, for many of them were beginning to claim that his cures were signs that the gentle young man had been chosen by Yahweh for a special purpose. Also, since Jewish tradition held that the Messiah would be of the House of David, Jesus, James and the others began to conceal their descent from David, in order to protect the family. If Miriam and Yusef had any misgivings about sending their eldest sons off on a long voyage to the Far East, political events changed their minds, and, once the Roman census was completed, in which Jesus was listed as "a son of Yusef the merchant of Capernaum, living at the Carpenter's House", Jesus and James sailed to India.

While being educated at Qumran, Jesus had read of Prince Siddhartha Gautama—Buddha. He was infatuated with the story of the rich and indolent prince who, driven by a deep religious urge, turned his back on his royal lineage and family and sat motionless under the Bodhi Tree, meditating and seeking enlightenment. This identification is understandable. Jesus, too, was of royal lineage, and, in fact, any member of his family had as much or more claim to the throne of Israel than did the sons of Herod the Great. Jesus felt a sense of divinity deep within him, making him dissatisfied with the world around him. Was he not, in his travels around the world with his uncle, seeking some kind of enlightenment?

What inspired Jesus most in this story was its result: the prince, Siddhartha, after sitting for years, was suddenly filled with a vision of divinity, and began to preach of the brotherhood of all men. The prince became filled with what was called the "Buddha-consciousness", and traveled far and wide, bringing his divinely-inspired vision of love and brotherhood to all he met. Jesus was also aware of what had happened to Gautama: before long, he became identified in the popular imagination with the Buddha, so that the man and the image of his indwelling god (which is what is meant by the "Buddha") became one and the same, and people began to worship the man and not his philosophy.

Also, Jesus had read the Persian tales of Zoroaster, another great religious thinker, whose life paralleled that of Gautama Buddha. Jesus apprehended that although each of these figures, with which he included his own existence as Akhnaton, appeared on the earth at different times and in different cultures, their lives and missions followed a common plan. Each came from noble lineage into a hidebound and corrupt society; each was driven by a vision of equality and brotherhood; and each brought to his culture a simple yet profound vision of "God" as indwelling, loving, and merciful. What's more, each taught that the world of outward appearances was an illusion that reflected and, sometimes, distorted the truth.

# CHAPTER TEN

# Jesus in History

MOST SO-CALLED "CHRISTIAN" teaching is based on corrupted texts and revisionist history. The remainder of this book will try to set some records straight.

It is important to note at this point that Jesus did not suddenly appear in Palestine presenting a new point of view. He was aware of many who preceded him, and was able to synthesize their teachings with his own beliefs, presenting a system of belief to his people that was specific to his culture, yet which embodied the same universal beliefs of the greatest epochs of history.

Those who have come this far in the recounting of the life of Jesus may have had many of their preconceived notions of the "biography" of Jesus challenged, and it is important at this point to take stock of some of them. From this point forward, many will be more familiar with certain aspects of the life of Jesus, and will be helped in their re-interpretation of his life by some clarifications.

The idea of the "Christ" was not new with Jesus. As we have recently noted, Siddhartha, at his enlightenment, was filled with "Buddha-consciousness". We should indeed not call Siddhartha (or Gautama) the "Buddha", but rather should make a real and crucial distinction: Gautama the man realized the Buddha within himself, and, after this realization, preached and taught from that Buddha-consciousness. That Buddha-consciousness is precisely the same force that Jesus came to know as the "Indwelling God", as revealed in his Essene education. Therefore, the reader will notice that there has been no reference to Jesus as "Jesus Christ". This is a misleading title, for it implies that Jesus was the Christ, rather than finding a Christ-consciousness within himself and proceeding through life from that frame of mind.

A distinction should also be made between the Messiah and the Christ. As we have pointed out in preceding chapters, the Jewish concept of the Messiah in Palestine was concrete and specific. The word "Christ", which seems to have become in history interchangeable with the word "Messiah", comes from a Greek word meaning "Anointed One". It does not, nor has it ever meant, "Son of God". "Christ", in the sense of "Anointed One", refers to "King", for kings were (and still are) anointed with oil at their coronations.

The Essenes taught of the "Son of Man", which they also called "The Teacher of Righteousness" and "Host of the Holy Spirit". It is in these terms and within this meaning that Jesus referred to himself as the "Son of Man". He uses this term often in the Four Gospels. Never in his life did he refer to himself as the "Son of God", but always as "A Son of God". It should be noted that the Essenes never hoped for a single figure to appear as the Teacher of Righteousness, as the other Jews awaited the appearance of the Messiah. They taught, and all believed, that the Teacher of Righteousness was the Indwelling God.

How Jesus came to be called "The Son of God" will be discussed and clarified at length in a later section of this book. Yet before we enter the period of his "ministry", it is important to plant in the mind of the reader that Jesus was never any more than a man. This does not mean that any time he was less than a man. This should be noted carefully, or, if it is not, the true teachings—indeed, the very life of Jesus—are wasted.

As a Jew, and specifically as an Essene Jew, Jesus never claimed to be divine. What he realized, and what he shared in common with his heroes (Gautama and Zoroaster), was the unlimited potential inside man.

The reader who has followed this rethinking of the life of Jesus may be wondering, "Is this book only out to de-mythologize Jesus?" In truth, this book is here to invite the reader to re-assess the life and teachings of Jesus, which have been so radically distorted throughout history.

It would have been unthinkable for a devout Jew in first-century Palestine to declare himself "The Son of God". If Jesus had ever done so, he would have been executed for blasphemy. Yet if he referred to himself in public as "The Son of Man", a phrase that was common to Essene thought, he would have been widely understood to be a great teacher. What Jesus discovered in himself was the Indwelling God of the Essenes, which can be called the "Christ-consciousness". In Aramaic (the dialect of Hebrew that Jesus spoke), there are no definite articles, so if Jesus referred to himself as "The Son of Man", it would have been recorded as "Son of Man". Likewise, if he referred to himself as "A Son of God", it would have been written down as "Son of God". A later translator, by interpolating "The" in both terms, could easily have named Jesus "The Son of God", to the exclusion of all others.

What Jesus knew and what he taught is that every human being—in fact, as he learned in Britain, every creature, animate and inanimate—is a "Son of God". All beings on earth are the creations of God, which was defined by the Jews as the angry, external god Yahweh, but which was known by Jesus and the Essenes as the creative force, the intelligence that forged the universe. What Jesus, as an Essene Jew, wanted to teach was the same lesson put forth by Akhnaton, Gautama, Zoroaster, and other great teachers of history: that all creatures are equal in the sight of God, which is to say when they are viewed from the Christ-consciousness.

If we define the Christ as the Indwelling God, then it could be said that each person has the Christ-spirit within him- or her-self. Jesus was a man, but a man who fully realized that Indwelling God. Although a later section of this book will examine the actual teachings of Jesus, we should remember that, despite all of the miraculous things attributed to Jesus, he said, "Whatever I can do, you can do."

In his travels, Jesus was taught the greatest wisdom available in his day. When he was taught by the great and visionary scholars of the Essene Brotherhood, these ideas re-awakened in Jesus the awareness of his eternal soul. Each person's soul was created simultaneously with that of Jesus, so indeed we are all equals with Jesus. His particular journey through time and the human race, through his various incarnations, was his journey, and his alone. Each soul's path is different, and leads through different times and experiences. Yet Jesus learned in his travels, his education, and, most of all, his experiences, that each soul's path leads to the same end, which is the realization that we are all God, individually and collectively.

In his travels to Persia, Jesus visited the many cities and sites attributed to the career and teachings of Zoroaster, also known as Zarathustra. Zoroaster lived in the sixth century B.C.E., and most of the religions of the areas now known as Iran and Iraq are based on the teachings of Zoroaster, although these were radically reinterpreted by Mohammed who, curiously enough, tried to reinterpret them with an eye toward "Christianity".

Again, many legends sprung up around Zoroaster, creating the image of a divine demi-god who could work miracles, but what Zoroaster actually realized was a system of belief based on cosmic laws. Zoroaster was a visionary and a seer who "saw" the forces that moved the planets. Today, much of what he saw in his visions is in the domain of science, but in his time, no one before him sensed the relationship between earthly beings and planetary forces. Today, this has been watered down into a childish, superstitious form of Astrology, but Zoroaster knew that earth was a specific place in the cosmos where many forces of divine energy converged.

In his visions of the cosmos, Zoroaster saw how huge bands of energy moved the planets, and created the dimensions to be found in our solar system. All in all, he sensed seventy-seven different dimensions of existence, each with infinite possibilities of beings. Because the earth is the third planet from the sun, which is the great vortex of energy that powers our nine-planet system, Zoroaster determined that our planet seems to be made of three dimensions, which create time, space, and light. He envisioned the sun as a vortex of energy no different than a chakra (see Chapter Six), and from this vision, saw that all beings in the heavens and earth are made from the same divine energy, shaped by the number of dimensions present. Hence, according to Zoroaster, since this world is of three dimensions, within light, space, and time are fused matter, mind, and spirit.

Following this train of thought, a one-dimensional system would create existence of only one factor, that of spirit; a two-dimensional system that of mind and spirit; and so forth. To follow this thought from one extreme to another, a no-dimensional system would be pure energy, while the cosmos reaches out into infinite dimensions. This vision was one of the greatest mystical systems ever codified, for although Zoroaster himself existed in the three dimensions we all share, he perceived that his truest self, his most indwelling self, was of infinite dimensions, and therefore was unlimited in its power and effect on the universe, which was the same as saying it was the power commonly ascribed to God.

In the ancient Persia of his time, there were many, many gods, most of them angrier and more vengeful than Yahweh. Zoroaster's vision, which was disseminated by him, his father, called Zend, and his son, called Zarestra, negated this polytheism with a vast, sweeping vision of divine energy and possibilities. For Zoroaster, each soul, each separate entity, possessed many dimensions and such power that, if realized, could create universes and destroy them. (It must be noted that, in his visions, he perceived seventy-seven dimensions, and theorized their reach into infinity. His sense of infinity created such awe in him that he was satisfied to stop seeking dimensions—fields of existence—at seventy-seven.)

Unfortunately, his vision proved both too mystical and too complicated for most people to understand, and although the system of teaching promulgated by his father and son tried to communicate this in simple and elegant terms, his teachings soon became cheapened into a theology under which man is subservient to the motions of the planets and the heavens—the opposite of what his visions proposed.

Yet enough of Zoroaster's original teachings and writings existed, and had been passed down through an elect society, that Jesus could study such in Persia. As in his other travels, he had been made receptive by his education in Qumran. Again, Jesus was introduced by his uncle into a so-called "Mystery School", in this case a small circle of women who had studied all of the extant writings of Zoroaster and had used them to guide their own meditative visions. These women were a highly intuitive group of seers, all psychically gifted, who had learned Zoroaster's techniques of seeing into the forces of the planets and were able to tap into the forces that surround the earth. In particular, these seeresses introduced Jesus into the reading of the Akashic Records.

Again, as in the case of the chakras, Hindu terminology will be used.

Akasha means, literally, "ether", and the "records" are supposedly the belt of energy that surrounds our planet and records the activities of man through time. While this idea seems far-fetched to many modern minds, few today have trouble believing the technology which can encode huge amounts of information electromagnetically upon a very small piece of silicon or magnetically charged material. As it is with magnetic tapes or disks, so it is with this "ring" of magnetic energy, upon which is "written" all events since the beginning of time. (For purposes of illustration and clarity, the process—and the analogy—has been greatly simplified.)

Clairvoyants who do "readings" for people or who trace "past lives" are believed to gather this information from the Akashic Records. This information, however encoded, exists for those who are willing to use it for helpful purposes. As given in the introduction to this volume, the information contained in this book is "stored" there.

Although Jesus understood the concept of these records, and though he was able to use them, however automatically, the Persian seeresses had made a life-long study of their use, and instructed Jesus into the free and unlimited access to these records for purposes of healing. As Chapter Six outlines, the Essenes would consult the past-life records of certain cases, and they did this by "tuning-in" to the Akashic Records. Starting from this Essene knowledge, the women in Persia showed Jesus that each person on earth, even total strangers, can be read as an "open book" to one who is always open to the flow of divine energy. They taught him how to open his mind to these energies, and also gave him a startling demonstration of how those same forces can be used for evil.

A wonder-worker in that same town, who had trained with these nine women, was using his knowledge to fleece people in the marketplace. He would presume to "tell fortunes" for money, and, using the Akashic Records, would indeed tell revealing secrets about his patrons, for he did have access to the truth about these souls. Because he told people things that they believed no one could know, people became afraid of this wonder-worker's powers, and he extorted money to keep such things quiet. One of the women sent Jesus to find this man, and told Jesus to pay for this service. The wonder-worker told Jesus things about several of his past lives (things Jesus had already been told by the Essene Anna), and Jesus was told to "tune in" to the man at the same time, and report back to the women.

Jesus told the women that, indeed, this man in the marketplace told the truth, but Jesus "saw" that, as a result of using this power for selfish gain, the man was being literally eaten alive by cancer, and had not long to live. The women told Jesus that it was the result of abusing a divine power. Although the power itself would not cause such devastation, the man, on a very deep level, knew he was abusing something sacred. While the man denied this on a conscious level, on the level of his soul he felt deeply guilty about his violation of such a sacred mystery, and was devouring his own body as penance.

Jesus then asked the women if this man could be healed. They replied that the man knew how to heal himself, and it could be done instantaneously, but that he would not change his ways, and would die soon in agony, for that was what he secretly wished to do. Through the instruction of these women, Jesus realized that the root of all disease is the tension between the soul and the body, as manifested in the mind. When the mind and the body act consciously against the inner divinity of the soul, the "Teacher of Righteousness", the mind, perceiving that tension, will create an illness in the body correspondent to the amount of guilt, stress, or tension those acts create against the knowledge of the soul.

Thus, Jesus learned the difference between true healing and "sorcery" or "magic", sometimes termed "witchcraft". The principles of using the divine energy are exactly the same, yet when performing healing, the mind and the ego of the healer are "neutral"; i.e., the healer is offering himself or herself as a conduit or channel for divine energy so that the subject may be healed. In "sorcery", the same principles are used, but the ego is involved, for the "magician" is using divine principle for personal gain, and this, over time, so violates the soul's knowledge of its own divinity that disease results.

After his time spent with these Persian wise women, having been initiated into the discoveries of Zoroaster, Jesus, along with James (who had not studied in Persia) and Joseph, sailed on to India.

Before tracing Jesus's travels and studies in India, which were conducted in Benares, the holy city of the Buddha, we should note that, in the legend of Zoroaster, obscure though it may be today, are the seeds of what became Christian legend. Zoroaster, soon after his death, was turned into a mythical figure, as was Buddha, and worshipped. The story of Zoroaster was blended with Mithraic mythology that was already ancient in Persia to create a myth not unlike that of the New Testament Christ-figure. Zoroaster was supposedly born of a virgin, worked untold miracles, was pierced in the side by a lance or spear, died, was buried, and three days later rose from the grave and was taken bodily into heaven. Jesus recognized this myth, for he had been taught almost exactly the same story in Egypt, as the story of Osiris.

In Benares, Joseph put Jesus with only one man, an old adept by the name of Yana. Because Jesus was familiar with Buddhist teaching, Yana instructed Jesus in highly advanced Yogic disciplines. Although Jesus had studied about the kundalini, here he was taught to manipulate this subtle energy through the chakras of his body, and to channel this energy wherever it was needed, either in his own body or in that of others. Along with this intensely physical training, Jesus was instructed about the laws of karma, and here Jesus and his teacher differed strongly.

Yana told Jesus that one had to accept one's karma, that the deeds of the past were the cause of all pleasure and pain in the present. Yana also taught Jesus his belief of denial of the flesh, of non-involvement in the physical world. From his highly enlightened perspective, new-filled with much practical learning, Jesus debated his teacher's views. Jesus, while agreeing in concept with denial of the world, still clung to the fact that the entire reason to be in a fleshly body was to experience pleasure and pain, and learn from those experiences. Moreover, Jesus asserted that, no matter what one's karma, no door was ever completely shut, no pathway ever blocked. Jesus asserted that anyone at any time could erase or bypass karma by a "leap of faith", a belief in one's own divinity as whole, happy, and secure in the divine forces of good. Such an overwhelming faith in the "Indwelling God" could erase any errors committed in any past or present life. Yana debated with Jesus in turn, citing many examples, but Jesus was able to counter each example with a personal experience of healing or restoration of wholeness. Yana conceded that the philosophy of Jesus indeed surpassed the system of belief he held. Although the name of the concept Jesus professed to him was named much later, we can recognize it as the "Law of Grace".

# CHAPTER ELEVEN

# The Law of Grace

ON HIS WAY BACK FROM INDIA, Jesus and James spoke much about the concept of the Law of Grace. As far as either of them knew, this was a new idea. Jesus was inspired by the mechanics of healing, which seemed to reverse the effects of karma, at least in the classical Buddhist sense of the word. James and Jesus talked at length about the difference between the concept of God in the various cultures they had encountered. In India, the God was indwelling, and this seemed in tune with their Essene teachings, yet for the other Jews in Palestine, Yahweh, all vengeance and wrath, was the common notion. In Britain, James and Jesus were introduced to a benevolent Creator-Father-Mother from whose thoughts all nature sprang forth, while in Persia God seemed to be a cosmic force, moving through and acting upon forces of the universe.

Joseph listened intently to all of this without response, then asked Jesus, "Who, then, is God? Is He any of these, or all of these? These Gods all seem to be different things, different beings. What of the many cultures

I've seen that have many Gods? The Greeks, the Romans. What about the Roman Emperors, who call themselves gods?"

Jesus thought deeply. After a long pause, he spoke. "Yahweh, the old man in the skies, seems to be like an angry father whose children have disobeyed him. This is not my God. Yet this is the God of my ancestors. The God I know doesn't seem to become involved in human affairs, so I don't think my God is someone out there looking after me. Yet I believe that my God moves in and through all beings, including myself. My God is merciful, my God is kind, my God forgives all transgressions." At that moment Jesus was struck with what he had said. "That is my God, the Creator of all things, who loves us dearly, who forgives us for anything we've done, and who will welcome us back to His Kingdom at any time, as long as we realize that we are one with Him, and not separate."

James commended Jesus on his flash of insight, yet remained cautious. "If you spread that around back home, you won't make many friends. The Romans are in charge of Judea, and Herod rules in Galilee. If you want anger and vengeance, there you have them. Just try to spread this word of love and forgiveness." Jesus grew angry. "But that is the truth!" he roared. James and Joseph burst into laughter. Joseph said, "Don't bite our heads off! We agree with you! Your brother is just warning you. Take it from me, our lands are in terrible times. Our people need such a vision of God. We need to believe that what is being brought down upon our heads isn't the wrath of Yahweh, but the doings of the Romans. If you can make that clear, you'll be a very dangerous man." Jesus sat silently, brooding on that notion. "Besides," continued Joseph, "your family has other matters in store for you." Jesus knew what he meant.

The travelers returned to Jerusalem, and while Joseph tended to his goods, the two brothers spent several days in that city before traveling north to Capernaum. They had been gone about seven months, and visited with many of their Essene friends who lived in Jerusalem. There Jesus learned that new buildings had been constructed over the ruins at Qumran, and strangers were living above the stones that once made up the compound of the Essenes. Jesus also visited the Temple, and found that the new Priesthood was in the control of Rome. Most of the old, upright High Priests had either been removed or died, and those who replaced them were increasingly corrupt. From close friends who were connected to the Temple, Jesus learned that the Roman Proconsul had demanded a percentage of Temple Gold as tribute, or he would pull down the Temple buildings themselves. Jesus was outraged. Through all the corruption of Herod the Great and the previous Roman governors, the Temple Stores and the buildings were still considered sacred. For Mutius to demand a portion of the Temple's treasury would surely bring riots.

Jesus also learned about the Zealots. Many former Essenes had joined the Zealot party, also known as the Zadokites or Sicarii. These were mostly young men who were angry at the occupation of the City of Solomon by the Romans, and were unable to tolerate the corruption of the Priesthood. The Zealots were calling for a bloody revolution in the streets. Although Mutius had threatened to execute the leaders of the Zealots if any rioting took place, at that time all members of the Zealots still were free. Many of the Essenes feared that fighting would break out in the streets at any moment, while others felt that before that was allowed to happen, Rome would recall Mutius and replace him with a more diplomatic Proconsul.

On their journey northward to Capernaum, James and Jesus were happy to be at a remove from the politics of Jerusalem, yet both brothers knew that, before long, they would be drawn into the sweep of history in that ancient city. "We must prepare ourselves," James told Jesus, "for the hard times ahead." "Many are calling them the Last Times," Jesus commented, "but they are only the beginning. They may well be the last times for Jerusalem, for I don't think things will stay as they are. But the time is coming for you and me to spread what we have learned."

James was concerned that Jesus would put himself in jeopardy by speaking bluntly. Jesus answered him, "Our God will protect us, as long as we follow the precepts that we have found in every system of belief in all corners of the world... 'Treat others as you would be treated' and 'Love your enemies as yourself'." James was skeptical, and Jesus, half-jokingly, challenged him. "We are about to ride through Samaria. You know that Jews are often ridiculed and threatened there. The Samaritans despise us, as most Jews despise them. Yet I believe that if you and I simply keep those thoughts in mind, those divine commandments, we will be treated like friends wherever we go."

And, true enough, wherever Jesus and James went in Samaria, they were made to feel welcome. Moreover, wherever they stopped, they were able to find Samaritans who had heard of the events in Jerusalem and were hungry for news. Jesus and James were sent from home to home by a network of Samaritans who wanted to hear news and would welcome Jews in their houses.

When Jesus and James returned to Capernaum, their father and mother welcomed them with a great feast. They were happy to see their brother Jude and their sisters Ruth and Miriam. By this time, Miriam and Yusef had two more young sons, Simon and Joses. Jesus spent many hours relating his new discoveries and tales of his travels. Because his parents had made many new friends, Jesus was asked over and over again to tell his tales, and little by little he began to tell people of the new picture of God that he was realizing, and found that the simpler, more ingenuous Galileans liked what they heard. It was difficult for many of these rural dwellers to accept the harsh rules of Yahweh, when they saw the abundance and beneficence of nature all around them. Also, while Jesus had been absent, his reputation as a healer had spread, and many ailing Galileans were anxiously awaiting his return.

Four months after he had returned home, Jesus received a visit from his family's friends from Bethany, the family of Zechariah. Old Zechariah had two sons, Lazarus and Iokanaan (John), and his daughters Miriam (Mary) and Martha. These were the oldest and dearest friends of the family of Yusef and Miriam, and Jesus loved them much. Other than his own brothers and sisters, only the children of Zechariah were able to understand Jesus at his own level. He spent many, many hours discussing all that he had learned with John, Mary, Martha and Lazarus, and they enjoyed debating law and scriptures well into the night, as friends do.

In John and Lazarus Jesus found curious and open minds, and in Mary he found more. She was gentle, shy, devout, yet intellectually sharp. Because Zechariah was an Essene, he raised his children along Essene guidelines, so his daughters were as well-educated as his sons, and were not given to the typically subservient, submissive attitudes common to Galilean women. While Martha was already betrothed, Mary had yet to be promised in marriage, and Jesus found her charming, intellectually nimble, and of such a kind, gentle and loving nature that he became extremely fond of her.

This did not escape Yusef and Miriam, and, because Jesus was nearing twenty, it was time for him to marry. According to Essene beliefs, twenty was the age for men and women to marry and begin a family, and there were few exceptions allowed. While marriages at that time were almost always arranged, the Essene parents never arranged a marriage without an attraction already in place.

Yusef and Miriam took their eldest son aside after the family of Zechariah had returned to Bethany, and asked Jesus if he would like to marry Miriam (hereinafter "Mary") of Bethany. He said that he would, and Yusef agreed that in two weeks he would travel to Bethany to arrange matters with Zechariah.

At this point, many modern-day Christians will express surprise, or even shock, at the idea of Jesus marrying. We shall stray from our story to comment on this event. From a strictly historical point of view, it should be shocking that Jesus was not married. For an adult male Jew to remain unmarried past the age of twenty, let alone thirty, as Jesus appears in the Gospels, would be an anomaly, to say the least. We must always remember that, no matter what he taught or how he behaved, Jesus was always a Jew. In order for his teaching to reach his fellow Jews, and for him to become an example to his brothers and sisters, Jesus had to lead a perfectly normal life.

Central to the teachings of Jesus is a symbology that identifies God as a loving Father, and Jesus and all men and women as the children of this Father. The simple, illiterate and pragmatic crowds that listened to Jesus would not have stood for such talk if the man speaking those words was not himself a father. Additionally, Jesus often refers to himself as "the bridegroom", and this, too, was the result of experience, not an empty symbol. Because Jesus was himself a loving husband and father, the crowds who recognized him knew him to be a good and upright man, gentle to his wife and firm yet forgiving toward his children.

The earliest books about Jesus, written before the fall of Jerusalem in 66 C.E., were unequivocal about the marriage of Jesus to Mary of Bethany. This was accepted as fact for almost three centuries, until the age of Constantine, who, curiously enough, was a Mithraic worshipper. The Cult of Mithras was a corruption of Zoroastrianism, and under the Emperor Constantine the "biographies" of Jesus were rewritten and recut to parallel the legend of Zoroaster. As we have noted above, the similarities were already great, but Constantine could not accept a Jesus who was married and had children, because the God Mithras, a transmuted Zoroaster, had never married. (Of course, the historical Zoroaster married and fathered children.)

In the time before the marriage, Jesus was prompted to investigate something that John the son of Zechariah had told him about. There was another man named Iokanaan (John), called a radical by some and a prophet by others, who was preaching to great multitudes. This John was an itinerant holy man, a former Zealot, who was traveling through the north, telling anyone who would listen about a loving God, and exorcising "demons" and forgiving sins in the name of this God. Jesus had to find this man.

Of course, this man is known today as John the Baptist. While Gospel accounts, specifically Luke, link the infant Jesus with the infant John, even identifying them as distant cousins, the two were not related. Although John had been a Zealot, he had struck out on his own, and was radical in his beliefs and his life. He had studied with a sect called the Nazorites, who were not unlike the Essenes, but who were genuinely ascetic. John was commonly referred to as a "Nazorite", though he was *sui generis*, one of a kind.

Jesus and his brothers and sisters went out to hear John preach near the Sea of Galilee. Although John spouted much Nazorite eschatology, telling that the Last Times were indeed at hand (a popular subject for sermonizing, sure to hold a crowd spellbound), Jesus recognized in many of John's words a mirror for the inner knowledge he had realized for himself. After John's sermon, many followed him to the sea, for John promised that their sins would be forgiven by God through a ritual bathing, which he called baptism. This was a common Nazorite belief. Jesus recognized the wisdom of this gesture, and, although he was not baptized that day, Jesus and his siblings waited until the last member of the crowd was baptized, and invited John to stay with them.

They took John back to the house in Capernaum, and Jesus discussed many things with John, including the rite of baptism. Jesus noted that the Essenes practiced ritual steam-baths for purification, and asked John about the Nazorite ritual. John told Jesus that most of the Jews he had met on his travels saw themselves as evil and sinful, and could not be persuaded about their own goodness without some ritual purification.

"It is all well and good for you Essenes to have a ritual bath in your fine homes," John said, "but for the poor people who come to hear me, they have no fine homes, no baths. Yet they want to be purified. Is not the lake or the stream every bit as good as your fine bath?"

Jesus took this to heart, for in his travels he had seen many poor people purify themselves in streams and lakes. He knew that the need for purity, for the washing away of supposed "sins" was deep in the character of man, who denied his own indwelling divinity. "If any simple ritual like yours can help a man forgive himself, then it is of immense value," Jesus told John. "I, too, wish to tell these good people what I have learned, and what you and I have spoken about. Yet I am afraid that if I speak to them, coming from the House of David, and from a wealthy family, they will not listen to me."

"This is a simple, humble house, and when you approached me, I did not know anything about you except that you were a good and kind man," John said to Jesus. "I do not think anyone would believe otherwise. Many people in this area have spoken to me about your work as a physician, and you are well thought of, yet no one knows your background. Come out with me tomorrow. I will cleanse you along with the others."

And so, on the following day, Jesus followed John to the shores of the Sea of Galilee. There, John spoke eloquently of the mercy and goodness of God, and the crowd followed every turn of his keen mind and simple phrasing. Jesus was surprised to hear that many of the ideas and perceptions he and John had discussed the night before found their way into John's sermon. After he finished speaking, John led the crowd down into the sea, and there John "washed many clean".

When Jesus came along in the line, John turned to the crowd and said, "Here is a good and decent man, beloved by God and his fellow men. Many of you know him. I have questioned him and found him to be pure of heart and spirit, yet there is none among us who is without need of forgiveness." With this, John baptized Jesus.

Although the Gospels record that the "Holy Spirit" descended in the form of a dove at the baptism of Jesus, this is a literal rendering of a symbolic event. Again, Jesus had been highly trained and had experienced many startling and miraculous things in his travels, yet he still thought of the act of forgiveness on a highly intellectual level. John realized this, which is why he recommended that Jesus be baptized. For in his immersion in the waters of the sea, Jesus no longer held the idea of forgiveness, but actually felt, through the simple but powerful ritual act before a crowd, a sense of forgiveness.

Under the water, Jesus felt a radiance rushing from the powerful hands of John through his body, and came out of the water shaking. John smiled at him and said, "You have felt God." At that point, Jesus no longer felt that grace was an idea. He knew that it was a reality.

(Note: although the Gospels record the baptism of Jesus as occurring at the River Jordan, it did, indeed, occur in the north. As with many other details of the life of Jesus, times and locations were changed to "shore up" the fulfillment of Old Testament prophecy. See Chapter Twenty-One for further discussion.)

# CHAPTER TWELVE

# Jesus Begins His Work

JOHN THE BAPTIST AND JESUS spent much time together, and during their long conversations John questioned Jesus about his mission. Jesus acquainted John with all that he had learned on his travels, and while John was intrigued, his question to Jesus always was, "What good will it do?" While Jesus had spent much time in his education, John wanted to know how Jesus was going to use his knowledge and abilities.

Jesus admired John. John was traveling through all of the provinces of Judea, Samaria, Syria, and Galilee, without any itinerary, without money, friends, or disciples, depending entirely on the generosity of those who welcomed him. And John, who had no possessions save the clothes on his back and a staff, never went without food or shelter, except when he had gone to Jerusalem. "In that city," he told Jesus, "there are too many false prophets and teachers, and people are all too involved with themselves and with the politics of the land to listen to one such as I am."

Jesus wondered why John was only interested in the poor and downtrodden, rather than the more politically influential. John told Jesus that he came from a family as prominent as that of Jesus, a family that was rather closely connected to the Priesthood of the Temple, but that John's ideas about God and about salvation, deliverance, and goodness ran counter to those of his conservative, political family, and so John had gone his own way.

First, John wandered through the deserts, using that time to examine in great detail every belief he had ever held. During that time, John had many visions, and a "still, small voice" began to speak to him. John referred to that voice as the "Holy Spirit", the voice of the Indwelling God. Having discarded friends, family, wealth, and possessions, John had determined for himself what was essential to life and what was extraneous.

"I do not recommend this for anyone else, nor would I encourage it for you," he told Jesus. "Yet I can tell you what I have learned. I know now that man has very few real needs. All man needs to survive is trust in the Divine Power of the Universe to provide all needs. I have observed that no creature on earth save man goes hungry, or wants. Somewhere, long ago, man decided that God did not love him any more, and that somehow we men were unworthy of God's love. Yet I have never seen anything, not a tiny bird or a blade of grass, that did not have all it needed to live provided by God."

"Yet we do not trust that we have the same divine right to exist that the merest blade of grass has. This is as true of the rich as it is of the poor. You ask me why I don't speak to the rich; it's because their possessions are used to barricade themselves from the simple joys of life. I speak to the poor because they have so little to lose, and so much to gain from what I have to tell them."

John told Jesus that, while he did not possess the learning or the natural healing skills of Jesus, he nevertheless was able to change the station of his followers by changing their minds. "We have a notion that God is angry with us, and that he punishes us for our misdeeds. Yet we also believe that we are the chosen people of God. This is all wrong. What I tell people is that all men and women are the chosen ones, that in the sight of God we are all equal, that we are all loved, and that we must be willing to believe that we have the same rights as anyone else."

"Those are dangerous words in our world," said Jesus. "Though I understand them, and I agree with you, to fill the minds of the poor with such ideas could create a revolt." John answered, "If that is what will happen, then let it happen." Jesus asked John, "What if that brings an end to your teaching? What will all those whom you have helped do?" John was silent for a moment, then turned and looked Jesus deeply in the eyes. "If I had the ability and the knowledge you have, nothing—not even death—could stop what I have to say. I am only one poor man who has had a glimpse of God. Had I your understanding, and your ability to reason, I could change the world."

With that, John arose, and headed toward the door, then turned back to Jesus. "Perhaps what I am telling the people is only the beginning. I am preparing the way for you." Then he left. For a long time thereafter, Jesus accompanied John on his travels around Galilee, and wherever he went, although he did not introduce Jesus to the crowds, he constantly alluded to "the one who will follow me, whose sandals I am not even fit to unlace."

Jesus was troubled about what John had said to him. All his life, Jesus knew that he had entered the world for a purpose, and that his life was to be used to teach his fellow men a great lesson, yet despite all of his training, Jesus was still unclear as to what he was going to do and how he was going to do it. All he knew was that he was still young—he was barely twenty—and that the time was not yet right. And, to be sure, he was soon to be married.

Unlike the marriage of Yusef and Miriam, which had been a lavish affair at the Qumran Essene community outside Jerusalem (see Chapter Three), the wedding of Jesus to Mary of Bethany was a simpler, "country" ceremony, in keeping with more modest Galilean traditions. Because the family of Jesus was living in Capernaum, and Mary's family was in Bethany, a common meeting-ground was located in Cana. In Cana was a large group of Essenes from Qumran, sheltered at the house of a woman named Judith, who was called "Judy". She was a large, cheerful woman who tried to keep all of the Essenes in the area apprised of each other's whereabouts and activities. Although she could not be called a "gossip", her house was a center of communications, news, and activities. She had a large, open house, built after the Roman fashion, with an open atrium at the center, and she offered her house for the wedding and the celebration that was to follow.

Mixed in among the Essenes were many simpler Galileans who were friends of both families and of Judy. In order not to offend those who were not aware of or tolerant toward Essene beliefs, an Essene ceremony was performed at daybreak for only the families and closest adherents, and a more conventional Jewish ceremony was held later in the day for the gathered friends. The rituals were performed with great solemnity; not so the celebration that followed. The Essenes were all aware that Jesus was destined for a special life, and so were inclined toward excessive celebration of this most sacred event in his life; the non-Essene friends, many of whom came to Jesus for healing and counsel, loved this kind man from the south and, so, were also happy to celebrate the marriage.

Before the wedding was performed, however, Jesus took Mary aside and recounted to her all of his thoughts and beliefs, and tried to prepare her for the possibility that, once he began to "preach" what he had come to tell people, their life could be thrown into violent upheaval. Jesus was not unaware that he held views even more "radical" and incendiary than John, and also knew that, unlike John, he would have to carry them into Jerusalem and, if need be, to the Temple itself. He wanted Mary to be prepared for all possibilities, and told her that if she was afraid of what could happen, she could absent herself from the marriage without shame. Mary countered that she loved Jesus, and had known for a long time what sort of life she might face with him. She was determined to follow him on every step of his journey, and not ever look back or regret her decision to marry Jesus.

It is one of the tragedies of history that this beautiful and loving woman's fame has been degraded, and in further chapters we shall trace how this came to be. Although it is stated in one of the Gospels that Jesus "drove seven devils" out of Mary of Bethany, in fact this refers to the fact that Jesus initiated Mary into mystery traditions, opening her seven chakras, filling her being with the same divine energy Jesus had known in his mystery school training. In the Gospels, Mary has been deprived of the crucial role she played in the work and teaching of Jesus, and women throughout history have been deprived of an object of admiration and respect through textual distortions. Suffice it to say for now that Jesus and Mary were considered spiritual equals at the time of their marriage, and each entered into their union as the highest sacrament a man and a woman may make.

In the Gospels that relate the story of the "Wedding at Cana", the fact is omitted (or, more truly, has been censored) that the marriage being celebrated was that of Jesus and Mary of Bethany. Yet enough clues remain to fit the pieces together. While Jesus supposedly attends the wedding as a guest, it seems from the story that survives that his mother was responsible for the entertainment and refreshment of the guests.

Also, it is at the marriage at Cana that the first "miracle" of Jesus is reported, although that, too, is a distortion. What actually happened is this: during the celebration, much wine was consumed, and, near sunset, most of the guests were very drunk. Much food was consumed, much dancing went on, and by the end of the day, no one was ready to stop the party. Yet the guests had drunk all of the wine, and Miriam was distressed that there was nothing left to serve the guests, not even water.

She came to Jesus, asking him what to do, for Yusef himself was leading the festivities and Miriam did not want to interrupt him. Jesus said to his mother that outside the house were several large jars of water, which were to be used for bathing. Miriam said that she couldn't serve bathwater to the guests, because it was "treyfa", or unclean. She wanted to find more wine somewhere, perhaps at a neighbor's house. Jesus said, "Mother, the guests have had quite enough to drink. Bring in the jugs."

Miriam had the servants bring the jugs in. Several guests looked askance at the water-jugs, knowing that Judy kept them for her bathing. Jesus turned to the crowd and said, "There is no more wine, yet here is a drink that will refresh you more than wine." A guest said to Jesus, "But that is to be Judy's bathwater. How can you expect us to drink from those jugs?"

Jesus smiled and said to the guest, "Why does it matter what the water is to be used for, when the source of all water is the same? This water comes from the same wells as your drinking water, and, what's more, it has been increased by the rain which God sends down to bless the earth. If God has used this water to bless his creatures, why should you refuse to drink it?" With this he offered a ladleful to the belligerent guest, who drank it down and remarked, "This is no water. I believe that the bridegroom has saved the best wine until the last, for it is so refreshing, now that I know it has the blessings of God."

With that, all of the guests drank, and were refreshed by the cool, clear water. They applauded Jesus for his sense and wisdom, for while drinking the water, most of them realized that they did not need any more wine. So while nothing as dramatic as "changing the water into wine" occurred at this "Wedding at Cana", something more important occurred, for the guests were taught by the actions of Jesus that anything that comes from God and is given for man's use is a Divine Gift, that there are no special "blessings" that make food or drink "holy" or "pure" (remember, most of these people closely followed Mosaic "kosher" laws as to food and drink). Jesus taught the guests at his own wedding that the ordinary things of life, including all people of any status, are "holy" when seen from the point of view of the Indwelling God, which can be called the Christ-vision.

So, indeed, a miracle did take place at this most reverent and lively wedding, for Jesus first began to teach publicly what he had felt and communicated to his closest and dearest friends. On that day it can be said that Jesus began his public life.

At this time it is important to speak of the "miracles" of Jesus. Jesus was spontaneously clairvoyant, clairaudient, and aware of many simultaneous dimensions of existence at once. We should understand, importantly, that all people are so. What made Jesus different was not his prior lives, or any abilities that are "special". What "gave" Jesus these powers is the fact that, throughout his entire life, he was always told that all of these powers were innate and possible. As a result, he never questioned these abilities and considered them normal. It is only when such powers are considered "occult" (hidden) or "special" or "extrasensory" that a division occurs in the mind. There is nothing "extrasensory" about such abilities. They are "sensory", part of the ordinary makeup of the human psyche. The only difference between those who do not use these powers and those that do is the belief that they can be used.

And yet, these powers are inert in most people until they are "awakened" in some manner. In the case of Jesus, he was trained from an early age in all such matters, and was encouraged in his use of such senses. Moreover, he traveled to many centers of learning, so that his abilities encompassed the greatest teachings and knowledge of many cultures. All of this was done so that when Jesus began to synthesize all of this knowledge and education with his own intuition, he would be able to become an example of a man who has fully realized the Divinity that resides in each of us.

Without such an example for us all to follow, we would still persist in our erroneous belief that some people were "special" and others were not. Ironically, over the centuries, that is exactly what happened, so that the intentions of the teachings of Jesus have been inverted, if not perverted. We shall examine his teachings in a new light, so that we may discover the original intents of Jesus.

# CHAPTER THIRTEEN

# Readiness

FROM THE TIME OF THE MARRIAGE of Jesus till the beginning of the events described in the Gospels is a period of ten years. Again, just as the Gospels are silent about most of the boyhood and adolescence of Jesus, they are equally silent about this period. In order to make it seem as if the "Wedding at Cana" and the baptism by John were the preludes to the "public career" of Jesus, this gap of ten years has been left out, but this period is in fact one of the most important and crucial times in his life.

Essene belief held that a man should be married at twenty and begin his active life in the Essene community at thirty, during which ten-year period he was initiated and educated into the teachings of the community. This roughly corresponds with the seven-year cycles of the chakras in the body, in which the life-force or kundalini fills each successive "wheel" of energy in seven-year increments. Therefore, the marriage year precedes the opening of the third chakra at twenty-one, just as the entrance into the "community" follows the opening of the next chakra, the heart, at twenty-eight. In fact, the years of marriage between twenty-one and twenty-eight were thought to be essential to the opening of the heart. (This time-frame existed for both men and women in Essene thought.)

Of course, by the time of the marriage of Jesus to Mary of Bethany, the Essene community did not exist as a physical community, but as a less formal association. Also, because of his extensive education and travels, Jesus was not to spend this time in training, but was able to use this time "gathering his forces". In the north country of Galilee, Jesus assembled a small, secret group of men and women who met, seemingly informally, at his parents' house. These people, most of whom were associated with the Essenes resident in Galilee but some of whom were country people who had become friends with Jesus and Mary, are remembered as the "Disciples".

Unlike the disciples of the Gospels, there were more than twelve, and the circle included not just men, but women as well. We must remember that the Essenes did not, in contrast to the general beliefs of the Jews at the time, separate men from women and consider women of lower status. The Essenes revered women as the embodiment of the feminine principles of the Indwelling God, just as the masculine was the other side or half. Yet, in order to introduce the teachings of Jesus to a more male-dominated world, later writers eliminated the women from the "Apostles" circle, just as they numbered the remaining men twelve, to represent the twelve tribes of Israel.

Soon after the wedding, Yusef, the father of Jesus, died. By that time, most of the family's business interests had been totally handed over to Joseph of Arimithea, and Jesus became, for all intents and purposes, the head of the family, responsible for the management of the family's money. As we have noted earlier, the family was well-off, although they did not live in a manner that led anyone to believe that they had a great deal of money. As Essenes, the family gave much of their money to others in need, taking only what they needed for themselves. At the time of the death of Yusef, the family was helping John the Baptist with his work, and was giving funds to the houses of the Essenes in Galilee who offered lodging free of charge to travelers.

During this ten-year period, Jesus began to formulate what he had been preparing for his entire life: his "ministry". Events in Jerusalem were changing quickly. As quickly as he had appointed Mutius the Proconsul of Judea, [the Roman emperor] Tiberius removed him, replacing him with Pontius Pilate. This was not a wise choice, for Pilate was quite corrupt, but, since he was willing to be paid off by the Priesthood of the Second Temple, Pilate was not likely to create the kind of destructive chaos that the Jews had known under Mutius. One of the reforms of Pilate was to restore the throne of the Jews.

Herod Antipas, son of Herod the Great, was the ruler of the province of Galilee, while his brother Philip was tetrarch of Syria. Herod Antipas struck a bargain with the politically astute Pontius Pilate, whereby he would move his court back to Jerusalem, becoming a figurehead of Jewish sovereignty, so that the people of Judea would feel like they had a king once again. Between them, Pilate and Herod devised a plan to effect this. Herod was to murder his brother Philip, or, to be more accurate, have Philip murdered; then Herod would marry Philip's wife, rechristen her "Herodias", thereby uniting and strengthening his ties to Syria; then he would move his court to the Royal Palace at the port of Caesarea near Jerusalem.

There was a small problem to be overcome: Herod the Great was not by descent of the Royal Blood of Israel. In order for his son Herod Antipas to become King of the Jews, the records that were kept in the Temple in Jerusalem had to be destroyed, thereby eradicating the true bloodlines of the House of David, and a fabricated genealogy was to be created so that Herod Antipas could lay claim to the throne. Pilate, having been bribed by the high priests to restore a vestigial monarchy, called in a favor, and had the genealogies destroyed and replaced with skillful forgeries.

It is this event, not commonly known, that was recorded by the Gospel writers as the "Massacre of the Innocents" by Herod the Great. Of course, such an event, as noted above, did not occur near the birth of Jesus. The record of that event, however, was written in "coded" language, incriminating Herod of the symbolic slaughter of the ancestors of Jesus.

Because of these events, Herod Antipas left Galilee and moved to Jerusalem. Jesus had remained in "hiding" during the time that Herod ruled Galilee, so that no rumors of a "Messiah" would lead the jealous tetrarch to suspect Jesus. Yet once Herod was installed in Jerusalem, one of his first acts was to assign spies to follow John the Baptist in his travels, for Herod suspected that if a "Messiah" was to rise to overthrow both the Romans and Herod's court, it would be John.

Since Herod Antipas was no longer directly ruling Galilee, Jesus began to heal and teach more openly, yet he still confined most of this teaching to private assemblies in the houses of his mother in Capernaum and his father-in-law in Bethany. Soon a circle of followers or initiates grew in both towns.

By this time, some readers may be wondering why no mention has been made of the town of Nazareth, since we are accustomed today to hearing the phrase "Jesus of Nazareth". In truth, the city of Nazareth did not physically exist until closer to the time of the destruction of the Second Temple in Jerusalem, about 70 C.E. Despite constant references to that town in the Gospels, Jesus could not have come from a place that did not exist.

This is a studied guess by writers trying to decipher events that happened in Galilee closer to the time of 70 C.E. As noted, none of the Gospels was written by anyone who was involved in the events, and errors were made in translation and interpretation. The phrase "Jesus of Nazareth" is a mistranslation into Greek of the phrase "Jesus the Nazorean", which was a term used in Jerusalem to identify Jesus with the Nazorean or Nazorite party.

During this ten-year period, Jesus and Mary of Bethany had three children. The eldest was a son, named Yusef after the father of Jesus. The next was another boy, named Nathaniel after Mary's grandfather. Finally came a daughter, who was called Miriam, after the mother of Jesus and also Mary (Miriam) of Bethany. (Note: the Essenes did not follow strict conservative laws of naming children such as are practiced today.)

Again, many will be startled to think of Jesus as the father of a family of children, but for three centuries such an idea went unquestioned; in fact, the descendants of these children and those of the brothers and sisters of Jesus and Mary were prominent throughout the history of the development of the early church. See Part Two of this book for more information along these lines.

While raising his family, teaching and healing, Jesus began to draw up a plan in order to fulfill his mission in life. He took his brothers James and Jude apart for several days, so that they could think about how best to conduct the business at hand. By now, Jesus realized that his "great demonstration", a public revealing to the people of Israel of the power of the Indwelling God over death, had to take place in Jerusalem, since that city was the spiritual center of the Jewish people.

Politically, too, events in Jerusalem made it imperative that Jesus preach there. As before, the Romans were in control of the city, but they were now collaborating with the priests of the Temple, the Holy of Holies, in supporting a puppet king. Herod had, of course, no claim to be the King of the Jews, and Jesus did. Yet, because of his education and beliefs, Jesus had no interest in becoming the temporal King of the Jews.

In those days of political unrest, it would have been possible for Jesus to raise an army of Zealots and storm Jerusalem, deposing or killing Herod and installing himself on the throne. Jesus knew that this would be futile, and had another plan in mind. Yet his plan could not be followed unless he did prove himself a rightful candidate for the throne of Israel. Here was the plan of Jesus, which shocked and startled his two brothers: Jesus was, at a given time which only he could discern, to enter Jerusalem in a symbolic way, fulfilling the prophecies of Isaiah. Isaiah predicted that the Messiah would enter the Holy City of Jerusalem riding on an ass, would be welcomed by multitudes, and would claim the throne of Israel.

Also, Isaiah predicted that there would be a forerunner to this entry, one who "cried in the wilderness", announcing the coming of this king. All of these events, as foretold by Isaiah, would be fulfilled by Jesus, so that the people of Jerusalem would begin to demand that Jesus be installed on the throne of Herod. Jesus would not, of course, demand this for himself. Jesus would be captured, tried as an insurrectionist by the priests and the Romans alike, be condemned to death, and be seen to die in a public place.

Then, Jesus would rise from the dead, also in fulfillment of the prophet Isaiah's words, and be seen to be alive. Again, although this startling sequence of actions would have political repercussions, once and for all Jesus would show the people of Israel how their God—their Indwelling God—could triumph over death, that physical death was an illusion, and that the soul or spirit, the part of God that exists within each and every being, can never die.

To be certain, Jesus would never have formulated such a plan if he had not already experienced a "death and resurrection" at a much younger age while in Egypt. By this time in his life, Jesus knew that time was an illusion as much as death, and that the spirit, the Indwelling God, had the power to restore and revivify the flesh as long as one believed in the infinite power of that force.

Jesus assured his brothers that he would know when to begin this series of events, and that for the time being they should all carry on with their lives. Jesus also felt that he should reveal this plan as soon as he had formulated it so that his loving family could adjust to the unfolding of events that would seem to result in the "death" of Jesus long before they were called upon to witness what would seem to be a barbarous execution. Needless to say, the members of the family were quite disturbed by what Jesus told them, but after the passage of a week, began to adjust to the inevitability of these events and saw the great wisdom of this plan.

Before daring such a public demonstration of his personal beliefs, however, Jesus embarked on a "trial period", during which he was to teach this system of beliefs to the generally illiterate and practical people of Galilee. He began by gently teaching all he knew and had learned to the circle of friends and relatives mentioned above. Because he had learned so much, Jesus was concerned that he be able to communicate all his ideas, which differed widely from the religious beliefs of the ordinary people, in such a way that the multitudes of Galileans could understand them.

During his travels, Jesus was exposed to many different versions of the same universal principles, and, because of his rigorous and open-minded education, he was able to absorb each version and synthesize them into an all-encompassing vision. Yet he knew that his countrymen, for whose sake he entered the world, did not have the same imagination or wide-ranging experience. Soon after Jesus began to teach the circle of Galileans, he realized that he had to couch his knowledge in the vocabulary and symbolism of the Jews. Intuitively, Jesus knew that he could not address these practical people in theoretical and abstract ways, so he found ways to use simple, homely illustrations to convey psychologically and spiritually complex notions.

While the fishermen and shepherds might have found it difficult to comprehend a lecture about the "Creative Divine Imagination" and "Indwelling God", as the Essenes did, Jesus discovered that they grasped the same ideas even better when they were couched in parables about God as "Loving Father" and "Good Shepherd". In a country suffering under the yoke of Roman domination, beset by famine and deprivation, Jesus could speak of a loving father-like God who provided sustenance and support, and people understood what Jesus meant.

Because Jesus had spent much time alone, traveling in the company of his brother James and his uncle, and studying alone, he often felt more comfortable in solitude than among people, and so it was necessary for him to learn to address crowds of people. He began with this small circle, teaching them in entertaining but stimulating tales and parables, and as he gained in confidence, he began to join John the Baptist when John was in the area. John often asked Jesus to address the crowd, which Jesus did with more and more aplomb.

Also, because he had spent so much of his early life alone, it was tremendously important for him to have the love of Mary and the children. Although we would like to think that Jesus was perfect in his vision, he himself knew that he needed to feel all the pleasures of earthly life, to know the riches of the marital union and enjoy teaching and playing with his bright, curious children. Jesus knew the dangers of living too intellectual a life. He also knew, through his dialogues with John the Baptist, that to live too ascetic a life was to falsely deny the pleasures of earth-bound existence.

Although Jesus greatly admired John, he gently teased the Baptist that he was no closer to God by denying himself such pleasures as good food and the joy of a loving family. John countered this by saying that "I must live as the poorest of the poor, so that they may listen to me without envy." Jesus smiled and picked a flower from the earth. "Tell me what God denies this flower that he would not have you enjoy." Jesus maintained that while one is in a physical body, one should temperately enjoy earthly pleasures, for when earthly life is through, there is enough time to experience other, less physical states of existence.

Both John and Jesus were aware that there were Roman and Herodian spies in the crowds wherever John spoke. Although those spies were difficult to detect, when "seeing" the crowds clairvoyantly, Jesus found it easy to detect which were genuinely listening to John and which were marking John's words in order to report them to their superiors. Often Jesus warned John about the dangers inherent in preaching so openly, but John was reckless, often coming very close to challenging these spies to show themselves. "My work is nearly done," John told Jesus, "so that yours may begin."

John was preaching and baptizing people near Jerusalem when he first publicly announced that he was merely the messenger for one who would follow him, and referred to himself in the words of Isaiah as "the voice crying out in the wilderness". At the same time, John began to denounce Herod. No one had dared to openly accuse Herod of poisoning his brother Philip until John did so, knowing full well that the reports would reach Herod within hours. The crowds listening to John's speeches were shocked at such a revelation not because they did not suspect such a crime, but because they knew that such a thing could not be openly suggested.

It did not take long before Herod sent a battalion of his guards to arrest John and imprison him. John went willingly, for he knew what was about to happen. As soon as the soldiers took the Baptist away, the people were ready to riot. While John had never encouraged his followers to use violence or take arms against the injustices of their existence, the people were quick to come to those conclusions. It was only the strong presence of hundreds of Roman soldiers on the streets of Jerusalem that prevented the crowds from an uprising.

When word reached Jesus in Galilee that his beloved friend John had been arrested by Herod, he knew that it was time for his work to begin. This was the sign he had been waiting for. All along, Jesus had begun to assemble many followers, many of whom are accurately remembered by the extant Gospels. What the Gospels do not record is that among his chief followers were his own brothers, sisters, and in-laws. He called the closest of these together and told them that the time was at hand for him to begin what he called the "Great Demonstration".

Before beginning such a journey, Jesus knew that he had to face himself, for if he embarked on such an adventure with any selfish motives, he could easily ruin what he had set out to accomplish. And so Jesus, following the example of John, bade his family goodbye and went into the desert wastes north of Galilee to meditate upon what he was about to undertake. Because of what he had learned in Egypt's deserts, Jesus did not take any supplies with him, for he knew that this was to be a time of purification. As the Gospels say, Jesus wandered in the desert for forty days and forty nights. He trusted that the supposed wastelands would provide enough food and water to sustain him, and Jesus also knew that he had to push himself to the limits of his endurance in order to face what was ahead.

Although, in the symbolism of the era, the Gospels say that Jesus was "tempted by Satan" in the desert, what Jesus was wrestling with was his own ego. Jesus knew that the power within himself could be used for personal gain and, like any man, he could turn those powers to selfish ends. He was, indeed, by bloodline and wisdom, qualified to become the king of the Jews. In truth, Jesus was tempted to do so. He knew that many people were trying to force John to follow the same path, and John could not claim such a right by birth.

In the desert, Jesus had visions of himself sitting in the throne occupied by Herod, ruling over the land. He also had visions of using his understanding of healing arts to become a celebrated wonder-worker. His knowledge of Jewish law and brilliant mind could have advanced Jesus to the position of High Priest, had he so desired. All of these visions Jesus entertained in the desert, and rejected. Had he pondered these possible futures for himself surrounded by the urban seductions of Jerusalem or the comforts of his wife and children, he might have given in to any one of these temptations. Yet in the vastness of the desert, which seemed bereft of life yet was teeming with God's creations, Jesus cast aside all temporal desires in constant prayer. By "prayer" it is not meant that sort of concerted effort that amounts to pleading with a god who resides "out there" in the universe, but going within to the Indwelling God, and listening to the "still, small voice" of what has come to be called the "Holy Spirit". It is this voice that Jesus identified with, the voice of his Divine Self, and not his ego.

When he returned from the desert, Jesus was prepared to carry out his plan, and had learned to trust only the voice of the Holy Spirit. In the parlance of some eastern religions, it may be said that the ego of Jesus "died" in the desert, but it would be closer to the truth to say that in the desert Jesus pledged all parts of his being, physical, mental, and spiritual, to the uses of the Holy Spirit, his Indwelling God. Any ideas Jesus held about God before going into the desert that were still intellectual or theoretical were, by the time he returned, ready to be put into practice. Jesus the man had fully realized the "Christ-consciousness" within himself.

Immediately upon his return, Jesus began to speak publicly. At first, he confined himself to the area around the Sea of Galilee, then began to range far and wide, though he still did not go to Jerusalem. On most of his journeys he was accompanied by his wife, Mary, and his brother James; often Jude, who could have been the "twin" of Jesus though he was much younger, went with him, too. The children of Mary and Jesus stayed with Miriam, the mother of Jesus, and their aunt Ruth. One of the most crucial friends to accompany Jesus was Mary's brother Iokanaan, who is the "beloved disciple" of the Gospel called "John".

This is not the place to enumerate in detail the "ministry" of Jesus until his entry into Jerusalem, for the Four Gospels, especially John's, report many of these accurately. Yet the events which occurred in Jerusalem require examination

# CHAPTER FOURTEEN

# The Entry Into Jerusalem

WE WILL NOT DISCUSS all of the events that came to pass in Jerusalem before the crucifixion, for, as with many of the events of the ministry of Jesus, these are well documented in the canonical Gospels. What must be dealt with are some of the historical discrepancies that occur in these accounts and, more importantly, the radical misinterpretation of these events.

Through the ages there has been a rumor, which has given rise to several major heresies, that Jesus did not undergo an actual crucifixion, but that a "double" took his place. There is another school of thought that says that Jesus did not actually die on the cross, but was drugged into a deep sleep so that he could be taken down and revived. If either of these cases was true, it would negate the actual purpose for which Jesus went through this ordeal.

What gave rise to the first story was the fact that the younger brother of Jesus, Judas or Jude, looked so much like his elder brother that he offered to take Jesus's place on the cross. This is the brother called

"Thomas", which is a corruption of the Greek "Didymus", which means "twin". More about Jude, or as he is sometimes called, Judas Thomas, will be given in the next section of this book.

It was crucial to the teachings of Jesus that he actually die through crucifixion and return to life. But what is not enumerated in the Gospels as they stand is the mastery of Jesus over the physical form. There is a tale of Jesus walking across water to meet some of his disciples who are in a boat. This is an example of Jesus appearing to his followers in the form of what is called in some esoteric literature an "etheric double", a projection in near-solid matter of an image of the physical body.

In reality, this "double" is a manifestation of one of the "subtle" bodies described in Chapter Six. Because of his training and healing powers (which, as stated above, are present in all people, though dormant), Jesus was able to manipulate the subtle bodies contained in his physical form. This is what allowed him to pass through the stone tomb in Egypt during his initiation.

This is also how many of his so-called "miracles" occurred. Since illness is a phenomenon of the body that is a result of the beliefs of the sufferer, sometimes a radical, rapid change in beliefs can cause what today's medical practitioners call a "spontaneous regression" or remission of a disease. While modern medicine foolishly regards such an occurrence as a "freak" incident, it is in reality an instantaneous healing caused when the patient suddenly no longer needs the illness as a manifestation of a dis-eased inner self.

Because Jesus preached to the crowds of a gentle, loving, all-caring father-God, many who lived under a self-imposed curse were spontaneously cured of such illnesses as leprosy and epilepsy (which was believed to be caused by demon-possession during the lifetime of Jesus). Those who believed in Yahweh as an angry, vengeful god feared that they suffered because they had transgressed the laws as they were given to Moses and the Prophets. Added to this was the notion that all mankind was cursed by the "transgressions" of Adam and Eve, and the murder of Abel by Cain.

As soon as a powerful, charismatic teacher like Jesus told his audiences that God (by which he meant the Indwelling Divinity) was a loving God, and that all sins were forgiven by this loving force, many people hearing these words no longer felt that they were cursed and punished by

Yahweh, but loved and supported by the Divine Imagination.

Of course, there were some whom Jesus did not or could not heal, and they, too, are reported in the extant Gospels. These are people who, for one reason or another, still relied upon their illnesses to manifest a message to themselves, and were not willing or able to release the illnesses. Jesus never maintained that he himself "performed" such miraculous healings, but that these miracles were merely illustrations of the power of self-forgiveness and the innate powers of the body and soul to perfect the human form.

One pertinent saying of Jesus that was not recorded in the Gospels is about the notion of sin. When asked by a Pharisee about disease as a punishment for sin, Jesus replied, "There are no sins. What you would call sins are merely mistakes. If your son, while learning to walk, falls and hurts his toe, would you take a knife and cut off the boy's foot? No, of course not. Because the boy did not sin, he simply stumbled. And because you are a loving father, you will pick up the boy, hold him to your bosom until his crying stops, and then set him back on the road so that he may learn to walk more. Why, then, do you think that God punishes you each time you stumble and fall? If you think of God as a loving father, you will know that each time you make a mistake, God will still take you into his bosom, and help you get back on your path of learning."

This saying was undoubtedly excised from extant scriptures because it makes reference to Jesus as a father of small children, which was unthinkable to those who assembled and severely edited the Gospels in the Fourth Century C.E.

Another celebrated incident in the career of Jesus in Galilee was the raising of Lazarus, brother-in-law of Jesus, from the dead. What is not told in this tale is the fact that after Lazarus died, and his spirit left his physical body, Jesus was able to actively dissociate himself from his own body, in what is often referred to today as an "out-of-body" state, and communicate with Lazarus.

Lazarus, ill with tuberculosis, had given up hope as his body became riddled with the infectious disease. After his spirit had left his body, Jesus was able to tell Lazarus that he did not need to die, and that if he stayed near his physical body for three days, and focused as much healing energy (for Lazarus had been trained by Jesus in healing arts) as possible on the body, it would be re-activated and mend itself. Those who feel that this is implausible should remember that the cells of the body continue to live for some time after the spirit departs from the flesh, eventually dying at their own rate. Lazarus was able, with the guidance of Jesus, to repair his frame, purge most of the disease from his body, and then return to flesh.

This sort of event is, as one might assume, not an everyday matter, but it occurs often enough in modern hospitals to be in common parlance today, labeled a "near-death experience". Perhaps this is the time to note that the reason many of the truths behind the legends of the healings of Jesus have never been revealed is because most people through the past two thousand years were not ready to accept such notions as the spirit leaving the body, the body continuing to "live" after "death", and such things as spontaneous remissions of diseases. Today, such occurrences are spoken about and understood by millions, yet no prominent theologian will risk his or her reputation to draw parallels between such natural phenomena and the work and teachings of Jesus. The most troublesome quotation of Jesus in the Gospels is one which states "Anything I have done and can do, you, too, can do and more." We are so used to a Jesus Christ who is the "only begotten son of God" who can work wonders that we miss the point of the statement above, which simply points the way to healings, miracles and forgiveness as natural processes.

Today, no one seems to believe that they are capable of the same actions and miracles as Jesus, yet we can read the Gospels and the "Acts of the Apostles" and try to believe that all of those semi-mythical figures were able to do such things. Why, then, do we not believe such things are possible? One possible explanation has to do with the misinterpretation of the most spectacular public act of Jesus: the crucifixion.

People in Jerusalem in the year 34 C.E. were no more willing to believe such things as most people are two millennia later, despite the fact that even more miraculous occurrences happen on a daily basis. Modern science has weakened the belief of the survival of the spirit and the healing potential of the body. Theologians and churchmen continue to preach about sin and evil, warning people against "Satan", even though psychology has taught us about the ego instead of a devil, despite the powerful teachings of Jesus about love and forgiveness.

This book has appeared now because the minds of so many women and men are more able to grasp some of the concepts and notions talked about by Jesus so many centuries ago. Despite the materialistic, scientific tenor of your age, millions believe in such events as are described above, and even your modern medical science, which has itself worked so many miracles, is beginning to rely upon the hidden powers of the body to heal itself; science is finding that the belief in healing is every bit as important as the mechanical processes of the body itself.

What has not been brought up to date, however, is the character of Jesus himself. After centuries of worship as a divinity, we have forgotten that Jesus was a man who realized within himself that he was God. The ancient Jews often referred to the Divine (who could not be named) as "I AM", and, it must be remembered, Jesus was a Jew. The "I AM" is perhaps the closest one can get intellectually to an understanding of what the force we call "God" truly is, for if one can say, "I AM", meaning, "I exist", then one can believe that one has always existed, and always will exist, despite one or many physical deaths, whether in a continuous frame of cause-and-effect time or in a series of simultaneous presents.

For "I AM" has no past or future. Anyone now reading this book is asked simply to turn his or her eyes away from the page and say aloud, "I AM". By saying this several times, one affirms his or her eternal existence. This is the one and only "mystery" of the universe. Through all his teaching and schooling, his travels and miracles, Jesus knew that "I AM" was the truth about the presence of God. All of his sayings and works were based upon the realization, which he felt so deeply in the desert, that "I AM" means "I AM GOD AS YOU ARE GOD". All who are alive at any time in the present tense are part of "All That Exists", and, therefore, are a part of the Divine Imagination.

Today, you can sit down and read such a discussion in a book like this, but in the time of Jesus, in 33-34 C.E., most people could not read. There were no books, no newspapers; the government of Jerusalem was militaristic and corrupt; the priesthood was equally corrupt and self-serving, caring more about appearances and the acquisition of wealth than teaching spiritual truths; the common people were taxed beyond their means, and there were many, many starving and homeless.

The only way for Jesus to communicate his ideas, radical in their time and perhaps no less so today if properly understood, was by some great public demonstration in the greatest of cities in Judea—Jerusalem, right under the noses of the Romans, King Herod, and the Sanhedrin.

Earlier it was noted that when John the Baptist was imprisoned by Herod, Jesus knew it was time to begin his teachings near Jerusalem. He spent almost three years in the area, waiting for another sign that he was sure would come, and, in 34 C.E. it did. Herod, who had kept John imprisoned, finally had him beheaded. The followers of John, during John's imprisonment, turned to Jesus for guidance and inspiration, for John had often told the crowds who came to hear him speak that another great teacher, one "whose sandals I am not fit to unlace", was coming, and that they would know him by his wisdom and purity of thought.

As we have noted, Jesus and John were not similar in their ideas about daily life, but they shared the same transcendent vision of a loving, forgiving God-force, and were both outspoken in their criticism of corruption and greed in the Priesthood of the Temple and of the King and Roman government. John, while in prison, had many visions about the future, in which he "saw" his own brutal execution, but he was unafraid, knowing that he, in his own way, was part of the revelatory teaching of Jesus. As long as John remained alive, Jesus knew that he could not enter the city of Jerusalem as a leader of men, but when he heard of John's murder, he spent the better part of a week mourning with his family and followers, then entered the city.

It was nearing Passover, and there were many from all parts of the provinces of Judea, Syria, Samaria and Galilee in Jerusalem. Pilate was determined to make a show of his force, and as a result there were countless crucifixions around the outskirts of the city. With so many grim reminders of the cruelty of Rome, the people feared death at the hands of tyrants. Yet political fervor was also at a high pitch. One of the followers of Jesus was Judas, not the brother of Jesus but the Judas that is often referred to as "Judas Iscariot". (This simply means that he was named Judas and was one of the political party called the "Sicarii", who were also known as Zealots.)

These Zealots had thought that John was the long-awaited Messiah who was to lead them from slavery, and were near to insurrection when John was beheaded. To dissuade them from taking arms against Herod's palace, the King had John's head placed on a spear outside of the palace, with a guard placed around it for a week, while John's body was thrown to the King's dogs.

This action outraged Jesus and his followers, who were lodging in

Jerusalem with many Essenes. Jesus and several of his party begged the guards to take down the head of John so that it could be buried. The Sicarii wanted John's head as a symbol of tyranny, but Jesus was able to convince the guards that he merely wanted to give what was left of his friend a reverent burial so that the head could not be used to foment a riot. Jesus and his disciples quietly buried John's head in the garden behind the town house of Joseph of Arimithea, who was also in Jerusalem for the holy days.

Although Jesus knew that John would die at the hands of Herod, he could not contain his anger over the brutal treatment of his friend. He and his family, including his brothers, sisters, and in-laws, were entering the public part of the Temple when Jesus saw the many tables of the money-changers and those who sold small animals for sacrifices. Because there were so many travelers in Jerusalem who felt obligated by Mosaic law to make sacrifices at the Temple, these money-changers charged unreasonable rates of exchange for Roman and foreign currency, and even more outrageous prices for sacrificial animals.

Jesus knew that the Priests of the Temple actually leased these spaces to the merchants, and took a percentage of their profits. Also, as an Essene, Jesus did not believe in the ritual sacrifice of animals. While he went to the Temple in a spirit of reverence, mourning for his beloved friend John, he became angry at the blatant commercial profiteering at the place which was considered the holiest site in the city.

Jesus's anger became uncontrollable, and he began to violently turn over the tables of the money-changers, freeing all the sacrificial animals, as reported in the Gospels. This story is told in the New Testament basically without distortion, yet it shows a man capable of great fury and outrage, who is unafraid to take action. Those who believe in "gentle Jesus meek and mild" have always had trouble with this violent action, yet when Jesus is viewed as a man, one with deep devotion and convictions, with love for his fellow man and his Indwelling God, his anger in the situation is understandable.

Yet Jesus was also aware of how such an action could help him in his mission in Jerusalem. While the Priests had him driven from the Temple and threatened him with arrest (because he was in the Temple of the Jews he was not subject to Roman authority), they could not punish him because of their own complicity in the profiteering and corruption which Jesus exposed to the people who witnessed the act. Moreover, word of the actions of Jesus spread like wildfire through the city, and before two days were out, everyone had heard of this zealous Galilean.

It was during this time that Jesus was called a "Nazorean" because of his affinities with John the Baptist, who belonged to that sect. Because of the time Jesus had spent traveling and in the northern province of Galilee, he was not thought of as a resident of Jerusalem or an Essene, but seemed to this city like a stranger.

## CHAPTER FIFTEEN

# The Crucifixion and Resurrection

WE NOW COME TO what may be the most misunderstood event in history. Jesus was arrested, tried, and condemned to death in Jerusalem in the year 34 C.E., as the Gospels report. Three days after many people saw him die in a public place, he was seen again, this time by many more people. Because his entry into Jerusalem was so public, and because of the scandalous act in the Temple described in the previous chapter, most of the people of Jerusalem knew about this man, and many were certain he was the Messiah.

Shortly after the Temple incident, Jesus left the city and encamped along the banks of the Jordan. Word was spread that Jesus was going to speak about the incident, and, because of his notoriety and his association with John the Baptist, nearly a thousand people came to hear Jesus speak. It was at this time that what has become known as "The Sermon on the Mount" was delivered. (Those who will compare this sequence of events against the Gospel accounts will find differences not only with this text but among the Gospels themselves.)

The feeling in the crowd was one of tense anticipation. Many—in fact most—of the people gathered were awaiting the words of a political Messiah, and many Nazorites and Sicarii were prepared to raise an army and follow Jesus into the city and begin a war of liberation. No one expected Jesus to speak so movingly of love and forgiveness, or against violence. What could have been an ugly scene became a demonstration of loving thoughts and the distillation of all Jesus knew and believed. Jesus and his party were well aware of the fact that the crowd contained many spies employed by the Romans and the Priesthood.

The next day, after this notable speech, perhaps the finest in human history, Jesus borrowed an ass from a friend who kept a farm near Jerusalem, and entered the city. As people heard of his arrival, they rushed into the streets to see this stranger, about whom it was said that he was the Messiah, or the King of the Jews. Many today believe that the prophecies of the Old Testament foretold this entrance into the city of Jerusalem. Jesus, however, was aware of these prophecies, and consciously drew the parallels to them—such as riding the ass into the city—so that the people would make an association with the prophecies of Isaiah.

The city of Jerusalem was abuzz with the word of what this extraordinary speaker had said in the countryside, and many roamed the streets trying to find him. Upon his entrance into the gates of the city, word spread from house to house, and soon great crowds blocked the narrow streets of Jerusalem. Roman soldiers, acting as police, broke up the crowds and pulled Jesus off his humble steed. A civil warrant for his arrest had been issued by the Proconsul, at the request of the Sanhedrin, who had no authority in civil arrests. The reason for the arrest?

Destruction of property in the holy of holies, the Temple, on behalf of the merchants and moneychangers who operated stalls there.

Many attempts were made to question Jesus, in the hope that he could be caught up in the transgression of either a Roman or Jewish law. He was thoroughly grilled by the members of the Sanhedrin, who examined him not only on his supposed "transgressions", but also on matters of Jewish law. It must be told that many members of the Sanhedrin had an immense curiosity about this man, who seemed to come from nowhere but was conversant not only with every aspect of Jewish law, but of the known world. Little went on in Jerusalem that did not come under the scrutiny of this important council.

What seemed more threatening than any claims of being the Messiah (claims which Jesus neither confirmed nor denied, merely asking the Sanhedrin, "What do you think?") was Jesus's defiance of observing the customary silence about corruption in the Sanhedrin itself. Those whose families were well connected—the family of Jesus among them—knew that the members of the Sanhedrin had lined their own pockets with the treasury of the Temple. Moreover, the Sanhedrin was paid by the Roman government to "keep things in line". More than anything else, the Sanhedrin and the High Priests feared anyone who could lead an uprising against their corrupt status quo. It seemed that Jesus possessed such a following.

It was not unusual for the Sanhedrin, if they discovered that a self-proclaimed "Messiah" was planning a revolt against their own ruling body or the Roman occupational forces, to turn that individual over to the Romans for punishment and, possibly, execution. In order to do that, however, the Sanhedrin had to find that the individual in question had transgressed Jewish law. That offense being proven, the Romans would "arrange" a set of civil crimes that would guarantee execution. In the case of Jesus, however, the Sanhedrin could find no instance where Jesus had broken a law he could not irrefutably defend. For every accusation that was made in the "trial" of Jesus, he was able to cite justification for his actions in scriptures, often sending the Sanhedrin's scribes scurrying about to look up the quotations he cited.

After a full day's examination, during which Jesus was found innocent of any violation of law, he was turned over to the soldiers of the Proconsul for prosecution of the civil charges of "destruction of property". A recommendation was sent to Pilate to "go easy" on the prosecution, lest Jesus rouse the crowds against the mutual corruption shared by the Sanhedrin and the Roman rulers. The High Priest recommended that Pilate make some kind of financial arrangement that would allow Jesus to offer a lifelong silence and self-imposed exile from Jerusalem in exchange for a residence in a far part of Judea and exemption from further taxation. In other words, the Sanhedrin wanted no hand in the execution of such a learned and popular man, but greatly desired his silence.

Pontius Pilate, however, was not willing to make such an arrangement. As Proconsul, his control over the province of Judea was constantly being tried and shaken, and Pilate was concerned that the people of Judea thought him too soft. He was, therefore, quick to condemn and execute anyone who could possibly be considered an enemy to the state. The case of Jesus perplexed Pilate, however, since the only public act that could be counted "criminal" was the destruction of Temple property. Even if Pilate had been willing to make some kind of silencing arrangement, as the Sanhedrin recommended, he was unable to prosecute Jesus under any count because his actions in the Temple were exempt from Roman law. Because of the give-and-take between the Sanhedrin and Pilate, involving many financial dealings that fattened purses on both sides, Pilate had made a public arrangement with the Sanhedrin to consider the Temple "off limits", much as the Vatican is to modern-day Rome. Jesus could not be tried for a civil charge by the Sanhedrin, but could not be tried by the Proconsul for an action that occurred in the Temple. Pilate, nonetheless, was unwilling to let Jesus be freed on a technical flaw in the Judeo-Roman legal system.

Pilate and Jesus met very briefly, during which time Pilate explained this apparent "loophole" in the law. But Pilate was prepared with a tactic that, he thought, could trip up this mild-seeming but potentially dangerous prophet. Pilate asked Jesus if he considered himself the Messiah. Since he was no longer in the Temple, Jesus did not answer according to scriptural lines, but instead asked Pilate what he meant by that term.

"You Jews are always looking for this Messiah figure to come and raise a sword against us Romans... to try to topple our rule. I'm sure you're well aware that we've executed many who claim to be that man. Tell me, and don't dissemble... are you that man?" Without hesitating, Jesus responded, "If that is what you think the Messiah is, then I am not that man." Pilate then asked Jesus, "Who are you, then?" Jesus answered, "The Son of Man, the same as you. And a Son of God, the same as you."

"I have heard some exclaim, and loudly, too, that you are telling people that you are the King of the Jews," Pilate asked Jesus. "Is that so?" Jesus said, "I make no such claim. But if I wanted to lay such a claim to the throne of Israel, I have more right to do so than the man who now sits there. But if I am a king and a ruler, my kingdom is not of this earth. It cannot be seen, or felt, or known by the five earthly senses. Yet its reality is greater than Herod's palace."

Pilate stood and strode away, calling the jailers who attended Jesus. "Take this man to Herod. He is no threat to Rome, but Herod may find him a threat to the sovereignty of Judea." Jesus was then taken to Herod's palace to await an audience with the supposed King of the Jews. (It is worth recalling at this point that Herod and Pilate were both equally involved in a conspiracy to conceal the lineage of Herod, by which Herod had no legal right to claim a kingship over his fellow Jews.)

Jesus dreaded this meeting with Herod, for he was still full of outrage over Herod's execution of John the Baptist. Because of the fact that Pilate found no reason to prosecute Jesus, and also because the Sanhedrin wanted no complicity in his execution, Jesus knew that by being sent to Herod's "city" palace he was being set up for charges of treason and insurrection. Jesus was taken to a small chamber far from the main throne room of the palace. Herod came to Jesus already in a fury, knowing well who this prophet was.

Herod knew of Jesus's association with John the Baptist, and had been kept well informed of what Jesus was saying about him in his teachings. After berating Jesus with a string of insults, Herod asked Jesus, "What right do you have to claim that you are the King of the Jews?" Jesus replied, "Who says that I am the King of the Jews? I do not." Herod asked Jesus, "Who are you, then? Are you the Messiah?" Jesus answered, "I am the Son of Man. I am neither murderer nor adulterer, neither false king nor false god."

Herod refused to answer this statement by Jesus, but instead screamed, "Who will remove this man from my sight?" Attendants came into the chamber. "This man has blasphemed in my presence. He deserves to die." Herod's attendants removed Jesus from the chamber and returned him to the Roman soldiers charged with guarding the prisoner, who took Jesus back to Pilate.

Pilate the proconsul visited Jesus in a holding cell. He said to Jesus, "Your king has sent an order condemning you to death. You have been charged with crimes against your faith. As you know, Herod will make these charges known all over Jerusalem. As an official of Rome, I cannot act directly on Herod's order, but if you return to the streets, someone will certainly kill you. The Sanhedrin simply wants you out of their sight. I have found you a reasonable man. I don't believe that you intend to overthrow us or Herod. But you now have many enemies in this city. Your own Sanhedrin recommended that I arrange some sort of exile with you. Is that what you wish?"

Jesus looked Pilate in the eye. "My concerns are not of your government nor are they those of the Temple. They should be the concerns of all men, Roman and Jew alike. Yet you will not see anything but that which meets your face. What care I of death, either at the hands of you or some hired assassin of Herod's? You behold my only temple, my body. My soul dwells within this temple, but this temple cannot hold it. I tell you, if you destroy this temple, in three days I will raise it up again."

"Do not speak to me in riddles," Pilate said. "I took you for a sane man, but now you speak madness."

"This is not madness, but the truth," Jesus responded. "If you do not believe me now, soon you will." Pilate left the cell.

Late that night, Pilate met secretly with the High Priest of the Temple, Caiaphas. Often these two had met when a would-be Messiah threatened to disrupt the status quo of Jerusalem. The result was always the same: death by crucifixion, often on false or exaggerated charges. Although looking at this event from our present time, we would like to think that Caiaphas and Pilate were troubled by condemning Jesus to death, that the debate raged through the night over this self-proclaimed "Son of God"; in truth, the two men reached a hasty decision: death to Jesus. For these two who had put so many to death, one more potential enemy to their respective domains was of little consequence.

It was determined that Jesus was to be executed for attempting to raise a rebellion against the Temple and the government of Tiberius Caesar. A proclamation was issued, as was customary, warning any followers or adherents of this criminal to disband and cease any further rebellion under threat of the same fate. Both Pilate and Caiaphas have been held in contempt for centuries as a result of their decision that night, yet each one felt he was doing what was necessary and politically expedient. Human life was of little concern to either. As far as they were concerned, the matter was closed. They did not expect what happened next.

Jesus was crucified on a place called Skull Hill (Golgotha), so named because it was often littered with the bones of crucified criminals. This place was outside of the walled city of Jerusalem where crowds would not gather. As such, it was a favorite place of execution for political prisoners because its location was not well known. Jesus went to his execution without agony or suffering, because he knew it was part of his "great demonstration".

Before his arrest and imprisonment, Jesus had arranged with his uncle Joseph of Arimithea that, if indeed he was condemned to death, Joseph should take his body and place it in a small stone tomb in the back of his villa. Usually criminals who were crucified were left on their crosses until their corpses fell apart, so Joseph would have to bribe certain Roman officials to be able to remove the body of Jesus soon after his death.

Myth and tradition exaggerate the agony of Jesus on his way to the crucifixion. It is true that he was marched to the site by Roman soldiers, carrying the horizontal beam of his cross on his shoulders. As was customary, he was flogged along the way by the soldiers, who took sadistic pleasure in torturing their victims. It is also true that he was crucified with two thieves, simply because it was expedient to do so. Yet there were no great crowds who followed Jesus through the streets of Jerusalem. Those few adherents who tried to follow were roughly shoved aside as the procession passed through one of the city gates, and were not permitted to follow.

What of Mary of Bethany and the children? For safety's sake, they had removed themselves to Mary's family's house in Bethany, and had taken Miriam, the mother of Jesus, with them. The followers of Jesus knew that after the crucifixion the Roman officials would be seeking out all of the family and "disciples" of Jesus, so almost all of them went into hiding until after the body of Jesus was buried. Then, slowly, they made their way back into Jerusalem, mostly under cover of night, and were lodged in the home of Joseph of Arimithea, whose villa was on the outskirts of the city, yet still within its walls. As he had previously arranged with Jesus, Joseph of Arimithea had bribed the Roman soldiers on the execution detail to remove the body of Jesus soon after death and remand it to him. Notoriously corrupt and corruptible, the soldiers were more than willing to comply. As legend relates, one of the soldiers did indeed win the robe of Jesus by gambling with the other soldiers at the foot of the cross.

Well before the events of these days, Jesus had gathered his family and closest followers to celebrate the Seder of Passover in a modest house in Jerusalem. This is what legend and tradition have called the "Last Supper". However, at that meeting, Jesus did not reveal the one who would "betray" him, for there was no such betrayal either by Judas "Iscariot" or Jesus's brother Jude. Instead, he revealed to all assembled that "something will soon occur to me that will seem to all of you to be horrible. Do not be afraid when this happens. All that you will witness has but one purpose, and that is to fulfill my mission in life. That which you most fear is an illusion."

One of the followers asked Jesus to speak more clearly. "I cannot tell you more of what is soon to occur, for then one or more of you will try to prevent this from happening. Believe as I tell you, that all of the events of the next few days will cause you great alarm. When you seek for me, you will think that I am gone from your midst. Yet I will never leave you. Be patient and pray for but three days, and I shall again be among you."

Jesus took the unleavened bread and wine of the Seder table and passed them around. He said, "We celebrate the freedom of our people from slavery. In the days of our ancestor Moses our people gained great wisdom, yet to this day we Jews have been enslaved in many other ways. Take this bread and eat of it, and drink of the cup that I pass. For I tell you that after three days you will be freed from another, more insidious form of slavery, and will come to rejoice in time at what will seem to be the worst that could come to pass."

Jude, fearing the worst, asked his brother, "Jesus, are you going to die? If that is so, then let me take your place. Most people say that we look so much alike that I could die in your stead." Jesus replied, "Where I am going no one else may go, and what I do there you are little prepared to commence. All of my life to this point has readied me for what I am about to do. When you all see me again, you will be better prepared to live your life in the security of the arms of the Great One from whom your life proceeds. Speak no more to me of this." He ordered his friends and family to leave Jerusalem swiftly and without drawing attention to themselves, and return three days after the end of the feast of Passover.

When Jesus died on the cross, it was swift. The Roman soldier who coveted his robe asked the dying Jesus, "What crime is it that brings you to this place?" Jesus answered, "No crime save that of telling the truth to those who will not hear." The soldier offered Jesus water in a sponge. When Jesus was near death this soldier, whose name was Gaius Curtius, took pity on him, knowing that the powerful Joseph of Arimithea wanted the body to bury in a private tomb, and pierced Jesus's side with his spear to hasten what would have ordinarily been a prolonged and agonizing death from starvation, exposure, and infection.

Well before an actual, physical death, the spirit of Jesus had left the body, just as he had done in the tomb in Egypt. In many ways, the release was easier since the physical body was in such torment, and the departure of the spirit means an end of pain. Freed from physical form, Jesus traveled in his "astral" body to his family, his followers, and to Joseph of Arimithea, assuring them that he was dead in physical form but very much alive in a spiritual form. Although the people whom he visited were not consciously aware of his visits to them, they "sensed" his presence and were at peace.

The body of Jesus was swiftly removed after sunset and handed over to Joseph of Arimithea and his servants. They took the body to a small stone tomb in the garden of Joseph's villa, and laid it on a slab, wrapped in white cloths that had been soaked in a variety of herbs, among them myrrh and arnica. As in accordance with the arrangement that Jesus and Joseph of Arimithea had made, a large stone was placed in front of the opening to the tomb and a servant was posted there as a guard. Gathering all of his Divine Energy, the spirit of Jesus began to focus a tremendous force toward his earthly body, healing the damage done by the crucifixion. As he had supposed, it took nearly three days to restore the body so that Jesus could "return" to habitation in that form.

While this was going on, Miriam the mother of Jesus, Mary of Bethany, the children of Jesus and Mary, and most of the closest adherents assembled at the house of Joseph of Arimithea, as mentioned before. As the dawn of the third day after Passover broke, this band of followers went into the garden to the mouth of the tomb. There they found the servant who had been posted as a guard sound asleep. Joseph began to berate the servant for falling asleep when a voice called to him, "Do not blame this servant. No harm has come to the tomb." Joseph and the others looked around, yet could not see from whence this voice had come. Angrily, Joseph ordered his other servants to remove the stone that covered the entrance. They were all shocked to find the tomb empty.

Joseph wheeled on the sleeping servant, now awake, angrier still. "How could you have let the grave robbers come and take the body? I trusted you to guard this tomb, and now Jesus is lost to us forever."

The same voice was heard by all in the garden, saying, "I said to you that I would never leave you, and so have I kept my word. Joseph, my beloved uncle, give me your robe that I may stand among all of you again."

Joseph took off his robe without thinking, and held it in front of him. Jesus stepped forward from the bushes and took Joseph's robe to cover himself. "I once said, destroy this temple and in three days I will raise it up again. Behold, you see my temple newly raised, and I am among you once more."

# PART TWO

## What Happened After
## The "Death" of Jesus

# CHAPTER SIXTEEN

# James and Jude Take Over

FOLLOWING HIS "RESURRECTION", Jesus swiftly went with Miriam, Mary, and his children to Bethany. Because of the lack of communication in those days, nothing was heard in the remote country about events in Jerusalem, so no one in Bethany knew of the trial and apparent "execution" of Jesus. For two weeks he kept to the house, regaining his former strength. Many of his adherents and disciples came to visit him, and soon he was able to go out into the world again. During this time, he traveled widely in the company of Mary, his wife, while their children were left in Bethany under the care of Miriam, Mary's sister Martha, and the two brothers of Mary, Lazarus and John.

Wherever Jesus went, he told his followers that he had indeed faced "true" death and returned after three days in the tomb. Before, whenever Jesus preached that death was simply an illusion and that the spirit lives eternally, people accepted this, if they accepted it at all, as simply an abstract concept. However, with a man before them who was crucified by the Romans and could point to the physical scars of such a crucifixion, who was buried and arose from the dead after three days in a tomb, people began to believe.

The people of Judea, however, still suffering under Roman domination (although the burden felt lighter in the north), took the message Jesus was teaching one step further: if Jesus could be condemned to die at the hands of the Romans, be legally pronounced dead, and return to life, what hold could the Romans really have over the Jews? This, it must be pointed out, was not the intent of Jesus's "great demonstration", for he wished only to show that man's greatest fear, the fear of death, which dominates most of our unconscious thoughts, was illusory; that the life of the body was transitory and essentially valueless, yet that the life of the spirit goes on and on. It was the intent of Jesus to make men aware of their Indwelling God. He never meant to make a political statement against Rome, yet that was how his suffering and resurrection were perceived in those heated times.

Although communication between Jerusalem and the north was sporadic and irregular, a network of communication was well managed within the scattered Essene community that followed Jesus. Over the next five months he and Mary traveled from household to household in many towns throughout Judea, meeting in secret with Essenes and talking of the mysteries of life and death, bearing true witness that death was not to be feared. From time to time, the family returned to their house in Galilee, where Jesus and Mary healed the sick and met quietly with friends and neighbors. In all of these travels, Jesus was careful to avoid coming too close to Jerusalem.

Though his supporters and adherents had scattered and disbanded, two of the brothers of Jesus, Jude and James, were laboring in secret to re-assemble the circle of students and followers of Jesus. They promised this circle that Jesus was indeed alive, showed them the empty tomb on the estate of Joseph of Arimithea, and promised them that Jesus would soon return to Jerusalem in the flesh to preach to them. Unfortunately, word of the resurrection of Jesus reached the ears of Pontius Pilate through some of his many spies, and Pilate met again with the leaders of the Sanhedrin.

Pilate presented Caiaphas with the rumors that Jesus was alive, and it turned out that the High Priest had indeed heard such rumors. Fearing that, if such rumors were indeed true, Jesus could lead another uprising against the Roman rulers, Pilate and the High Priest tried to come up with a plan to discover the truth. Pilate was in a difficult position, for he could not under any circumstances condemn a man to death a second time after the man had been pronounced dead once before. Moreover, Caiaphas, remembering rumors from the past that such a Galilean had raised another man from the dead in Bethany, claimed that anyone who could rise from the dead was an affront to Yahweh.

Learning that James and Jude were still living in Jerusalem, Pilate sent spies to locate these two and bring them before him. In the same chamber of his palace where he had interrogated Jesus, Pilate grilled James and Jude as to the whereabouts of the body of Jesus. "He was buried in the tomb belonging to our uncle Joseph of Arimithea," James told the Proconsul. "I am aware of that," said Pilate, "for I caught the soldiers who turned over the body and had them flogged. By law a criminal's body must remain on the cross. Surely your uncle knew that. This is some sort of ruse to raise a rebellion, isn't it?"

Jude replied that there was no political motive in the removal and burial of his brother's body, and reassured the Proconsul that he and James were not assembling any kind of army. "Then tell me about this Messiah of yours," sneered Pilate. "Has he come yet? Isn't your brother thought to be such a Messiah?" James and Jude looked at each other, then James spoke. "My brother never claimed such a position for himself. He spoke of our God, ministered to the poor, healed the sick, and meant harm to no man."

"But he was seen committing acts of vandalism in the temple. You cannot deny that," Pilate said. "That was hardly an act without consequences." James spoke forcefully: "That was an act of outrage against the corruption of the Priests of our Temple, which is of no concern to the state of Rome. Unless you are willing to admit that you have more than a passing interest in the affairs of the Temple, I can't see where any actions that happen therein which do not affect the general peace of the city of Jerusalem should cause you any problems in your governance here."

Pilate dismissed James and Jude, but made certain that they were followed wherever they went. They sent word to Jesus via the chain of Essenes that kept track of his ministrations to avoid Jerusalem for as long as a year, or even until Pilate was recalled to Rome. It was not long before members of the Sicarii, who did indeed have a political agenda to topple the domination of Judea by the Roman empire, convinced the governors of the Roman provinces that Pilate was deeply corrupt and should be recalled to Rome. Such a recall did occur within a year, and Pilate's successors, of which there were no less than seven over the next three years, were too concerned with other matters of state to even recall the episodes surrounding the supposed "resurrection" of an itinerant Galilean who was merely one of hundreds executed during the reign of Pontius Pilate.

Because James had undergone much of the same mystery school training as Jesus on their travels, James was determined to keep the teachings and philosophy of his brother alive in the city of Jerusalem. He initiated Jude into those teachings, and eventually formed a mystery school of his own in the house of Joseph of Arimithea, who was frequently away from the city on merchant voyages. One of the men who was close to Jesus in Jerusalem was a fisherman whose nickname in Greek was Petros, meaning "rock", perhaps in reference to his burly physique. One of the earliest followers of Jesus, Petros—better known as Peter—had remained in Jerusalem and was a faithful devotee of the message that Jesus proclaimed of the Indwelling God.

When James and Jude realized that it was dangerous for them to remain in Jerusalem, they handed over the day-to-day operations of the mystery school to Peter, who, it appeared, had a talent for organization, and traveled to Galilee to visit with their brother. By this time, Jesus and Mary had established a very similar mystery school in Galilee, and day after day more and more disciples of Jesus joined him at this encampment. In addition, Lazarus and John established a similar school in Bethany. All of these schools were devoted to teaching what Jesus had learned before his crucifixion, and, most importantly, taught the great lesson demonstrated by Jesus after the crucifixion.

As can be imagined, by the constant telling and retelling of the story, small details were added and exaggerated by the teachers and students, until the persona of Jesus began to take on proportions greater than that of the actual man. Spending time in Galilee with Jesus, James and Jude reported such to Jesus, who instructed them to travel to the other learning centers and set the record straight. Jesus did not want his own personality to become the focus of the teaching, for he knew that such a development would draw the focus away from the reality of the Indwelling God that exists in each and every person.

"Persuade all of the teachers who are spreading our good news," Jesus said, "to concentrate on what I am teaching here myself. Stress to all of them that what I am and who I am is of little relevance to the teaching. All I have done has only been to teach them to realize the greater parts of themselves, to awaken their own divinity and let it guard their lives."

Jude wanted Jesus to travel with them, so that he himself could instruct all of the teachers that were spreading this philosophy, but Jesus told him, "That will only make matters worse. You see how people come to me for miracles, and are disappointed when I only speak to them. This disillusionment lasts for a long time, until they realize that whatever I can do, they can learn to do as well. If I suddenly appear, everyone will want to know what it is like in "The Land of the Dead", how I survived my crucifixion, and they will miss the lessons of what I am here to teach. It is better that I remain here and work in quiet, and that my teachings are spread without me."

"Then set down your teachings in a book, so that we may have it copied and sent to all those who want to follow you," said James. "My brother," Jesus answered, "you know from our travels together that learning does not take place in the pages of books, but in the hearts and souls of our fellow men and women. Besides, would you have me set down on paper what cannot be known in words? Such a document would be of no practical use and can be used against us. Many in Jerusalem think me a dangerous man, and you have been cautious in not seeming to organize any group that could be taken as a secret army. My way is face to face, and let it be your way as well, lest Rome perceive us to be their enemies."

Back in Jerusalem, Peter's gifts for organization were far outstripping his ability to teach. While James and Jude were away from the city, Peter was expanding the group that met at the villa of Joseph of Arimithea, establishing smaller groups at the houses of many prominent citizens who were sympathetic to the teachings of Jesus, most of whom had been Essenes. While Peter's efforts had been in earnest, his focus was precisely what Jesus had feared would happen: Peter dwelled more on Jesus the man than on his teachings, and began to proclaim that Jesus was indeed the Messiah, chosen by Yahweh to symbolically lead the people of Israel from "bondage" to freedom.

Such meetings attracted more and more people, and it did not take long for word of these meetings to reach the Sanhedrin. Soon spies infiltrated each of the groups, and the High Priest kept close watch on this movement, since it seemed that the followers of Jesus were becoming another revolutionary sect like the Sicarii.

A further problem was created by the simple nature of Peter himself, who began to enjoy the role of leader. Unaware of all of the political dangers of taking this fledgling movement into a public sector, Peter began to invite people openly to attend his various group meetings. Although he had been initiated into many of the teachings of Jesus by James and Jude, Peter became careless about secrecy.

James and Jude were in Bethany when they received word that Peter needed them in Jerusalem. They arrived in the city to find that Peter had allowed spies from the Temple to infiltrate their group, and learned that Peter was under arrest for organizing an insurrection. The brothers found Peter imprisoned in the Proconsul's palace, and once again called upon their uncle Joseph, recently returned to Jerusalem, for a favor. Joseph went to the ruling proconsul, a weak and ineffectual man named Silvio Frescius, and bought Peter's freedom, claiming that the fisherman and his followers were employees of his shipping business who had tried to take over his business while the master was away. Frescius was the sort to believe anything that had a bribe attached, and so Peter's freedom was easily bought.

Peter had learned a valuable lesson, however, and did not advertise his recruitment. It was scarcely necessary, for many Jews who had been hoping for a new, pure, uncorrupted way of worship took to the simple and understandable teachings of Jesus. Under the guidance of James and Jude, Peter leaned more heavily on the teachings and less upon the personality of Jesus. Joseph suggested that Peter take a short sabbatical and travel to Galilee where he could spend several months with Jesus himself, and offered to pay Peter's expenses. While Peter was on his way, a greater threat to the future of the movement begun by Jesus appeared in Jerusalem.

# CHAPTER SEVENTEEN

# Saul Arrives in Jerusalem

S AUL WAS A JEW who was born in Tarsus in the Roman province of Cicilia, beyond Syria. His father was a Pharisee who settled in Damascus as a result of his trading, and Saul's father became affiliated with the Roman forces occupying Syria, supplying them with grain and cheeses. When Saul grew to adulthood, he, too, became employed by the Romans, first as a paymaster, then as a tax collector, and finally as a procurer of goods for the Roman military. Like many of the Pharisees in Tarsus, Saul saw no problem in working for the Roman occupation, since there seemed to be no evidence that the Romans were leaving the Middle East in the immediate future.

Saul had worked his way up as high as a Jew could go in the Roman government in Syria, and when the Proconsul of Syria was transferred to Jerusalem, he took many of his closest workers with him, Saul among them. This Proconsul, Arcturus, took over the government of Judea and Jerusalem in the year 37 C.E. Saul, who spoke Latin and Greek better than he did Aramaic, was put in charge of requisitions for the Proconsul's palace guard. As he had been in Syria, Saul (who also went by the Hellenized name of Paul) served double duty as a spy for the Roman Proconsul.

When Arcturus took over, being the seventh successor to Pontius Pilate, he was briefed about the potential trouble to be had from the rebels. To demonstrate how well organized the followers of Jesus had become in less than three years, among the dangerous rebel factions were those led by Peter. Although there was no evidence of any uprising or military action from this group, the Romans considered them especially dangerous because they could not be bribed or successfully infiltrated.

Peter, after the time spent in Galilee with Jesus, had returned to Jerusalem as an exemplary leader. His ego, while still needing occasional soothing, did not get in the way of his administration of the teachings of Jesus, and he himself began to gain strength as an inspired teacher. James and Jude, when they were in Jerusalem, commented favorably on the progress that Peter had made.

As the Romans changed proconsuls and governors repeatedly, most of whom were corrupt and all of whom were incompetent, more and more Jews of all religious backgrounds sought to overthrow the Roman rulers. Since the time of the crucifixion and resurrection of Jesus, no less than ten uprisings had tried to retake the government of Jerusalem and had been put down by the Roman forces, resulting in countless crucifixions and public executions of the rebels. In a mere three years, executions were actually performed within the city walls as a warning to the Jews to obey Roman domination.

During this time the emperor Caligula came to power. Under Tiberius, who was by virtue of his position as emperor considered a god, the Jews were not forced to obey Roman religion but were allowed to worship in their own temple (controlled as it was by the Romans). Caligula, in his unchecked madness, demanded that all residents of his empire worship him publicly. Throughout the empire, including the city of Jerusalem, many images of Caligula were posted, and the residents of the city were obliged to fall to their knees before them and proclaim the divinity of the Emperor. Needless to say, this edict did not sit well with the Jews, and many revolts came out of this, which explains the constant changing of governors and proconsuls.

In addition, in the year 36 C.E. Herod Antipas, the puppet king of the Jews, was poisoned in his palace. Ineffectual though he was, Herod did hold sway over the treasury of the Temple, and the Sanhedrin was answerable to him in all matters of Jewish law.

What with the changes of local government, the whims of a mad emperor, and the poisoning of a despised Jewish king, the land of Judea was in disarray. When Arcturus took over, he was determined to know where the radical and revolutionary sects were, so he sent Saul of Tarsus and other spies out to infiltrate them. Among the first of the groups chosen by Saul was the followers of Jesus.

Unlike the Pharisees, Sadducees, Sicarii and other well-organized groups, these followers did not have a true organization or even a name. Peter, in his addresses to the meetings in various houses around Jerusalem, referred to Jesus as "the anointed one", a title which Saul recorded in his diaries (kept in Greek lest the Aramaic-speaking Jews of Jerusalem discover them) as Chrestos. Hence, the first reference of Jesus as Chrestos or Christ came from Saul. In his reports to his superiors, Saul gave this group the unofficial title of "Christians".

Saul was a learned man, a wise and crafty man, but one who was given to hiding his true nature from himself and others. Much speculation has been made about Saul from the letters that are in the New Testament, some of which are from Saul's hand and some of which are forgeries and distortions. Deep within himself, Saul longed for spiritual depth, honesty, and purity. However, he was a homosexual, which in those days meant ostracism from the sect of the Pharisees. So, as a result of the times and his culture, Saul had to keep his sexual identity a closely guarded secret, and pretended to be uninterested in either men or women sexually. We must remember that in the Jewish culture of the period, sexuality and love were hardly linked, and the notion of romantic love and marriages for love are a much later invention. As a result, sex was rarely (if ever) discussed, and in most sects, the Essenes excepted, men and women were quite often separated in public and dealt with each other according to strictures and laws that dictated behavior.

Saul was not alone in his homosexuality, but the Jewish culture, like Queen Victoria, did not acknowledge that such a phenomenon as homosexuality even existed. This may account for Saul's embracing of the Greek culture, which openly acknowledged and accepted homosexuality as part of human existence and behavior. The Romans were unofficially tolerant of homosexuals, while officially barely acknowledging their existence. Saul was suspect in the Pharisee culture of Tarsus for growing to adulthood without marrying, so he welcomed a transfer to Judea.

Forced into concealing his true nature by his native culture, living a life of "hiding", Saul was a perfect spy for Arcturus. He was able to fit into the Jewish culture of Jerusalem, but was also able to communicate and understand the Greeks and Romans who passed through that bustling city. He was also more than willing to tell everything he had learned to his Roman superiors.

Although Saul infiltrated several groups active in Jerusalem, he himself was most interested in the group he called the "Christians". James, Jude, and Peter initially accepted him into their circle, little suspecting that he was a Roman spy, although James was more than a little suspicious of this Syrian Pharisee who showed such interest. In truth, Saul was deeply affected by the message that the teachings of Jesus conveyed: the brotherhood of all men and women, the communal sharing of money and food by the group, the open acceptance of non-Jews into the circles, and many carry-overs from Essene teaching. Because he was a scholar, Saul recognized the influences on Jesus of Egyptian, Indian, and even Celtic studies. Fascinated that any single philosophy could embrace so many ideas and yet remain pure and simple, Saul the spy found himself becoming Saul the convert.

Saul began to reveal information to the Romans selectively, for fear of exposing himself as embracing this "Christian" teaching. Although the first "Christians" carefully avoided politics, urging their members to pay taxes as required to the Roman tax collectors and abide by Roman law (with the single exception of failing to openly worship the Emperor Caligula), Saul found himself telling his Roman superiors that the "Christians" would not accept the divinity of Caesar and were organizing to remove all effigies from the city—a blatant lie.

It is difficult to understand Saul's motives for telling such lies and more that followed, but it is only part of the picture to say that he felt guilty embracing the very school of thought that he was sent to observe and destroy. The Proconsul Arcturus was well pleased with Saul's reports, and put the Syrian Jew in charge of a Roman battalion that was to seek out and destroy the members of this sect. It must be said that Arcturus sent reports on to the Sanhedrin, claiming that the circle headed by Peter, James and Jude was a radical and heretical sect.

Back in Rome, the grandson of Herod the Great, called Herod Agrippa, was being educated and, although known as a royal Jew, became more Roman than the Romans. In a fit of paranoia, the self-proclaimed god Caligula ordered all Jews in Rome to be killed, but before this mad order could be carried out, Caligula was himself killed and his shy, crippled, stuttering but brilliant uncle Claudius was made Caesar. A modest, thoughtful man, Claudius tried to restore some sanity to the Roman Empire. One of his first moves was to send Herod Agrippa to Jerusalem to rule as king, knowing that Agrippa would preserve the Roman order at all costs.

Agrippa soon became the ruling force in Jerusalem, and the persecution of the Christians that was proceeding under Arcturus ceased. All effigies of Caligula were removed from the city, and, at the order of Claudius, they were not replaced. Some order returned to Judea, but Agrippa grew bored with the administration of the land, and slowly turned more and more duties over to the proconsuls. As before, the proconsuls of this time were corrupt and inept, and since they knew that the new king of the Jews was a Roman at heart, felt that they could raid the Temple treasuries at will.

The Zealots and Sicarii, learning of this, raised another siege, and were swiftly put down by the efficient and ruthless Roman soldiers. Before this time, at the feast of Passover in 41 C.E., Jesus returned to Jerusalem for the first time since his ordeal there, meeting secretly with all of the groups that convened in his name. Word spread rapidly through the Christian community that its master teacher was in the city, and after the feast of Passover Jesus slipped from the city, never to return again.

During his visit, without Jesus being aware, he was seen and heard by Saul at a large gathering at the villa of Joseph of Arimithea. At that time, Saul was out of favor with the rapidly changing Roman authorities, and, while impressed with the simple, honest, and penetrating stories and lessons taught by Jesus, he envied the adulation heaped on this great teacher by those whom he loved and who loved him.

Before leaving that gathering, Jesus said to his followers, "Though you, my people, are as gentle as lambs, you should be as wise as serpents, since among my lambs there is a wolf, ravenous and jealous. Be wary, and from this time forward, do not meet in groups larger than twelve, lest you be thought to be forming an army against our oppressors from Rome. Meet in secret, and do not greet each other in the street as brothers and sisters, as you do here in private. For I tell you the time will come when we will not be welcome in our own homes, and we will try to disown our own brothers and sisters to save ourselves. You who own property, sell it, and give the money to our brotherhood, for I tell you this, the time will come, and it is not far away, when all of us must leave this holy city, for even the Temple of Solomon itself will be destroyed. I speak not in parables now, but tell you of events that will come to pass. Fear not, for I who have died and returned to life am here to tell you that the love our great Father and Mother God has for us will keep us as a shepherd tends his flocks, lovingly but with a firm staff when danger is near. Those of you who see me tonight will see me no more in Jerusalem, for I am going to a high place. Those of you who will be called to join me will know when to come. The rest of you should prepare for the time when you leave behind all material things and find new homes for your physical selves. For know this: your true home, the home of your soul and spirit, are within the Kingdom of God, where no harm will ever befall you. And know this: whenever two or more of you are gathered in the name of the Holy Spirit that informs our lives, there will I be with you."

# CHAPTER EIGHTEEN

# Saul Storms the Kingdom

A FTER LEAVING JERUSALEM, Jesus went to Bethany, where Mary and the children were visiting her family. He spoke at the mystery school there that was led by Mary's relatives, bade them goodbye, and, with his family, traveled to his house at Capernaum in Galilee, where he sold the house and belongings. Along the way, he officially disbanded the mystery schools, admonishing the members of the circles to meet in private and be ready to uproot themselves, much as he did to the groups in Jerusalem. Gathering a small band of followers from Bethany and Capernaum, Jesus and his family, including his mother Miriam, moved south to the walled city of Masada in Idumaea, beside the Dead Sea, wherein a large and active Essene remnant lived.

Back in Jerusalem, James and Jude helped their uncle Joseph of Arimithea quietly liquidate his business, closing his trading routes around the world and selling his fleet, retaining only two small ships for personal use. By this time (44 C.E.), the number of "Christians" were counted in the thousands, and Peter saw to it that the teachings continued in smaller groups, appointing a number of "deacons" responsible for over-seeing the teaching in these small, covert circles.

In the Roman sections, rumors about this "Christian" group were rife. It was said that they worshipped a devil who had once been in earthly form but rose from the underworld and walked the earth half-man, half-fiend. It was said that this devil could not be killed. It was also rumored that these "Christians" sacrificed their children and practiced group sexual orgies.

Herod Agrippa, now King of the Jews, with his practical Roman mind, found that Saul of Tarsus, who had once been a Roman informer, was still resident in Jerusalem and sent for him. Saul told Agrippa that he did indeed know much about the Christians. He immediately set all the horrible rumors straight, but told Agrippa that they worshiped the God within themselves and would have no other gods. Herod Agrippa asked Saul, "Do they worship Yahweh as most Jews do?" Saul replied, "They do not sacrifice to Yahweh as they should. They do not believe in such rituals. They live in secret, and look forward to the end of the times as foretold by their prophet who indeed rose from the dead."

"Who is this man?" asked Agrippa. Saul replied, "They call him the Chrestos—the Anointed One. Some say it is he who should be King of the Jews."

In his mind, Agrippa marked this sect as heretical and dangerous, and restored Saul to the position of power he had once held. Saul was ordered to find the leaders of this sect and bring them before the Sanhedrin, where they could be tried for heresy. Saul was overjoyed to be back in favor, and saw that he could ingratiate himself to the new King, thereby cementing his position with the new administration.

Immediately, Saul had James, Jude, and Peter arrested and brought before the Sanhedrin. James and Jude were questioned first, and admitted that they were brothers of Jesus. They told the Sanhedrin that they did not know the whereabouts of their brother, which at the time was true. (Soon after, the Sanhedrin sent riders to Capernaum only to find that Jesus and his family had vanished without a trace—or at least that is what the close-mouthed community there told strangers.)

Peter was then called in, and all three were questioned about the fine points of the law, and it was determined that in no substantive way were the followers of Jesus heretical. The members of the Sanhedrin found them no more radical or troublesome than the Zealots or the Sicarii. Still, some of the older members of the Sanhedrin remembered vividly their examination of Jesus, and were surprised to learn that he was alive and well, even though he could not be found. They determined, in private, that this sect was potentially dangerous, especially if the sect's spiritual leader was able to rise from the dead and raise the dead, and so had the Roman legions flog the three "Christians" before allowing them to return to their homes.

While Peter, James, and Jude tried to warn all of their circle, Saul began to bring the deacons in for examination before the Sanhedrin. Of course, Saul knew who all of these people were, and stole into the home of Stephen, the eldest of the deacons, in the middle of the night and summoned him to the Temple.

Unlike the other three who had been before the Sanhedrin, Stephen was not a diplomat. A builder by trade, Stephen was blunt and passionate. He had learned of the examination of Peter and the two brothers of Jesus, and once before the tribunal, Stephen's temper flared. He began to denounce the members of the Priesthood of the Temple as hypocrites, growing rich from the offerings of the poor, fatting themselves on the animals that were sacrificed to Yahweh while thousands lived in poverty in the shadow of the Temple itself. Stephen shouted to the assemblage, "Our prophet has said that the day will come when this Temple will no longer stand, and the Jews will no longer live in the city of David and Solomon."

Without hesitation, the Sanhedrin found old Stephen guilty of blasphemy and turned him over to the Roman soldiers in the employ of the Sanhedrin, who took the old man beyond the city walls and stoned him to death. Conferring with Herod Agrippa and the ineffectual Flavius, now Proconsul of Judea, the High Priest stated that the Christians were a threat to the peace of the city, and recommended that they be routed from Jerusalem. Agrippa stated that, as King, he would have no official part in the persecution of any Jewish people, and recommended that Flavius, in the name of Rome, should "remove" the criminal element. Flavius, only recently arrived in the city, had no knowledge of where to find any of these people, so Herod Agrippa recommended that the program be put under the administration of Saul of Tarsus. To pay for the program, Flavius requested from the High Priest that a large sum of money be paid out of the Temple treasury.

Saul had accompanied the Roman soldiers to the stoning of Stephen, and upon his delivering a report of the murder to Agrippa, Saul was told to report to Flavius to begin arresting the Christians. Since Peter, James, and Jude had already been tried by the Sanhedrin, Saul could not arrest any of them, but he and the soldiers granted for his use began to visit the homes of the Christians by night and imprison them.

The close-knit Christian community heard of this and, remembering the words of Jesus before he left Jerusalem, began to steal from the city by night. Many families, carrying what they could on their backs, had to use whatever money they had to bribe the guards at the city gates to allow them to pass. Those who had relatives in outlying towns went to stay with them; some went to the communities at Bethany and Capernaum; some traveled to Egypt, where they were taken in by several mystery school sects; still others traveled as far as Damascus in Syria, where the community of Jews was large and the refugees could fit in without drawing much attention. Joseph of Arimithea, with the two ships he had not sold, offered passage for many of the Christians, sending one ship to the north and another to the south. Peter and his wife went on the northbound ship, Jude and his wife and children on the southbound, to join Jesus in Masada. James chose to stay on in Jerusalem to fight for the imprisoned faithful.

While this report of the dispersion of the followers of Jesus seems hasty, it did in fact occur over a period of about ten years. During this time, many rebellions arose and were put down, none of which were led by the Christians, although Flavius tried his best to pin the blame on them. When it was discovered that Flavius made a habit of raiding the Temple treasury, a riot of immense proportions broke out, and the streets of the city of Jerusalem resembled a battlefield for a period of more than three months. Many Christians languished in prison awaiting trial while the Roman judicial system was clogged with the trials of the leaders of these rebellions. Many, many Jews were crucified in the streets, many were stoned to death, and still many more rebels were murdered in secret. Most of the Christians were merely forgotten until the rebellions were quashed.

Saul, however, was unceasing in his persecution of the Christians. Over the years, he learned that a large group of Christians had assembled at Damascus. Since he was raised in Damascus and knew the city well, he took a small group of spies and traveled north to Syria.

Jesus, now nearing sixty, continued to teach and heal the sick at Masada. His followers protected his identity zealously, letting only the true initiates know who he was. By now he was legendary, and many Christians felt it necessary to leave the lands of Judea by way of Idumaea so that they could be blessed by the prophet himself. It was during this time that Miriam, the mother of Jesus, died and was buried at Masada. Joseph of Arimithea, her brother, now an old man, had come to stay with her, and provided for her tomb.

Jesus was kept well informed of the persecution his followers were suffering under Saul. He kept himself removed from active participation in any actions, but often, in a so-called "astral" state, would visit the leaders of the far-flung circles of followers and appear to them either in dreams or visions, advising them of actions to take. The two sons of Jesus and Mary, Yusef and Nathaniel, now grown to manhood, wanted to take arms and travel to defend their fellow Jews from the machinations of Saul, but Jesus told them, "Saul of Tarsus is our brother. He does not believe that there is any good in him, but inside his being is the same spark of our Mother-Father God that is within us. Leave Saul of Tarsus to me."

While traveling to Damascus, Saul and his men had stopped at an oasis for the night. His men had gone to sleep, but Saul was troubled with his customary insomnia. Suddenly, in a burst of light, Saul saw a man standing before him, a figure not of flesh and blood, but of spirit. The men who were sleeping around him were completely unaware of any presence. Saul could not take his eyes from the radiant figure before him. This was, of course, Jesus projecting his form to Saul. "Who are you?" Saul said, not aloud, but silently in his mind, addressing the figure before him. "You know too well who I am," came the answer, "and I know who you are. Saul, Saul of Tarsus, why do you persecute my people? Are they not your people as well? Did I not warn you years before in Jerusalem to close your ears to the evil voices within you and open your heart to the love that is God? Look deep within yourself, Saul, and see what is there. When you have seen deeply enough, you will know who you are and who I am, my brother."

The vision of Jesus faded from Saul's inner sight, and Saul fell to the ground in a great cry of pain and agony. This time, his men awoke and found Saul unconscious. When they awakened him, he screamed, "I am blind! I must look within! I will not see again until I know who I am!"

Saul's men took him on to Damascus, and on the journey Saul languished in a near-coma. He would not answer to the name of Saul, but only to his other, Hellenized name, Paul. Upon their arrival in Damascus, Paul, in a burst of energy, broke away from his companions and ran through the streets. Although the spies who took Paul to Damascus searched high and low for him, they could not find him. They reported to the Roman governor of Syria, who was technically the superior of the proconsul of Judea, that Saul of Tarsus was missing and could not be found.

But found he was. A Christian named Zechariah (not the father of Mary of Bethany), who had left Jerusalem eight years before, found the blind and half-mad Paul in a gutter and took him to his own house. Not knowing who this man was—he answered only to "Paul"—Zechariah nursed him and, along with other Essene-Christian followers, healed Paul's blindness. His sight restored, Paul related his entire history, the fact that he had been a Roman spy infiltrating the Christian communities, confessing to the stoning of Stephen, and relating the appearance of Jesus to him on the road to Damascus.

Zechariah and the others, bound by their faith to love their enemies, did not shun Paul, who seemed truly repentant for his former deeds. Paul wept openly that some of those whom he had persecuted had taken him in and healed him, and vowed never to raise a hand against the Christians—the very sect he had named—as long as he lived.

Paul remained in Damascus for two months, hiding in various houses, and was taught by Zechariah and others what they were spreading throughout the Jewish community in Damascus: the very teachings of Jesus that had drawn the spiritually hungry Saul of Tarsus in Jerusalem years before. Many wanted to meet this man, for few could believe that such a transformation could happen. Paul began to tell the Jews in Damascus that it was Jesus who brought this transformation, and that Jesus had chosen him to spread his teachings throughout the known world. Unlike many of the Jews who had heard the teachings in Damascus, Paul had indeed seen Jesus in the flesh as well as in a vision, and many there in that city began to believe what Paul said. After two months, a much changed man returned to Jerusalem. His goal? To settle matters with James, the leader of the fledgling church in Jerusalem.

# CHAPTER NINETEEN

# Paul's Personality

PAUL ARRIVED IN JERUSALEM to find the city much changed. For one thing, warrants were out for his arrest, for he himself had been charged with subversive activities. This was not unusual, since many who served as spies for the Roman government and then deserted were charged with imaginary crimes, given false trials, and executed. Few of these men were caught, for few of them dared to venture back into Judea once they had deserted. Because of his illness, Paul was changed in appearance. His hair and beard, which he had kept neatly cropped and dyed black (hair dye being used liberally by the Romans), was now straggled and grey. In addition, he now answered only to the name Paul. His Syrian accent drew little attention, and he was careful to conceal his former identity.

Because of his traumatic conversion and subsequent psychosomatic blindness, Paul was indeed a changed man. His impact on the course of Christianity was immense, for from the time Paul returned to Jerusalem through the fall of that city in 66 C.E., what was a loose organization based on the teachings of a highly advanced but humble and self-effacing man became an organized personality cult. For that reason, it is important to examine the personality of Saul/Paul in some detail.

As noted above, Paul was homosexual, a fact that caused him dismay in the Jewish culture of the time. However, little else save some cryptic comments in the true Epistles of Paul can be attributed to that fact. Of more importance was the fact that he was by birth a Roman citizen, having inherited that birthright from his father. As a result, Paul was educated in a Roman rather than a Hebraic fashion. His father and mother, while Pharisees, were more closely aligned with Roman ways and thinking. Moreover, he was educated by several Greek philosophers who were resident in Damascus. By the time he moved to Jerusalem, Paul was deeply uncertain of his own identity as a Jew.

While in Jerusalem, Paul had tried to learn more about Pharisaism and studied with the venerable teacher Gamaliel, but found that because of his cross-cultural prior education he could not understand or accept the laws and concept of Yahweh. While Paul did not believe in the pantheism of Rome or Greece, neither did he subscribe to the monotheism of the Jews. Also, growing up in Damascus, he was steeped in the mutations of Mithraism and several other Sun-God religions of Syria.

What came of all of this was a surface cynicism that masked any true religious feeling. Paul did not feel that he belonged to any cult or religion, and convinced himself that he was happy that way. His cynicism showed in his willingness to ally himself with the Romans for material and political gain. While the Roman proconsul and officers who ruled Jerusalem were politicians of the coldest and crassest sort, Paul was determined to outdo them all. As a result, he did not hesitate to betray anyone whom he met if it caused him to rise a step in the hierarchy of the Jews who collaborated with the Roman occupational forces.

What all of this ambition masked, however, was a deep insecurity and yearning for knowledge. Try though he might in private, Paul could not achieve any mystical powers or transcendent insights. He was a deeply divided man who kept almost entirely to himself and took pride in being devoid of love or compassion, while secretly longing to be loving and compassionate.

When he began to infiltrate the beginnings of the Christian church, he was deeply struck by the genuine fellowship and communal love exchanged in these circles of followers of Jesus. He found himself accepted without question by most of the Christians (with the exception of James, as noted above), and felt himself feeling genuine emotions of love and charity toward his fellow men, emotions which he had consciously tried to remove from his waking psyche.

As an intellectual, Paul was unable to rationalize these feelings with the cross-cultural religious training he had previously received. Also, as he began to love and respect those whom he had come to betray, his hardened heart began to feel a division of guilt, another feeling which he was unable to fully analyze. All of this psychological conflict took the form of an intense hatred of the Christians.

What Paul could not synthesize in his mind he converted to anger and loathing. Drawn as he was to the message of Jesus, Paul was unable to give in to his yearnings, and transformed his attraction into betrayal and punishment. Paul was never the sort given to seeing an issue from several sides, but rather was one who went "all the way" in one direction or another. Since he would not allow himself to follow the teachings of Jesus, he tried to see to it that no one else was allowed to do so either.

After his encounter with Jesus on the road to Damascus, Paul's tortured psyche inflicted a form of blindness on itself. As is often the case with a life-transforming incident, a deep depression and a dramatic physical illness or catastrophe causes one's former life to stop cold, so that a period of healing, both physical and emotional, can follow. Paul's recuperation in Damascus under the care of Essene-Christian healers forced him to examine the deepest questions of identity that divided his soul. By the time he returned to Jerusalem, Paul was indeed transformed, but, as is also often the case, he who is transformed in such a way becomes over-zealous.

When the best thing Paul could have done for himself would have been to quietly join a less-prominent circle of followers of Jesus and slowly and patiently learn his lessons, Paul presented himself to James, confessing all of his former transgressions against the Christians. He expected to be accepted by James and the others without question, as he was accepted in Damascus.

James, who was fully aware of the treachery of Saul of Tarsus, found it difficult to accept this new Paul into his inner circle. While James did his best to try to forgive Paul, by using his inner sight he was able to ascertain that Paul was still psychologically unstable and was not in a position to be entirely depended upon. Using this insight as guidance, James assigned Paul to one of the group's finest teachers, a man named Simeon. Paul was to spend a year under the tutelage of Simeon, learning the teachings of Jesus as they were being disseminated by the Jerusalem church. Paul was determined to become Simeon's best pupil, and Simeon prayed deeply that he might be able to teach this former persecutor without prejudice.

Paul learned of the teachings of Jesus, but seemed to be more interested in the man himself. In time he won the trust of Simeon and James, and often asked James to recount as many stories as possible from his memory about his brother Jesus and their travels and studies together. With surprise, Paul learned that the family of Jesus was of royal blood and could claim a clearer right to the throne of Israel than the descendants of Herod. Despite his conversion, Paul's brilliant analytical mind tried to discern why Jesus never sought the Kingship of Israel.

James told Paul, "The Kingdom which my brother seeks is not the Kingdom of the nation of Israel, but the Kingdom of God. To be sure, the nation of Israel lives more in the hearts of the men and women of Israel than it resides in a palace in Caesarea. By making us aware that the true Kingdom of God lives eternally within us, my brother serves God more faithfully than if he sat on the throne of power in Herod's palace. There is more spiritual power and energy in the soul of a simple fisherman, if properly channeled, than there is in the strict, hidebound interpretation of the law of the High Priests of the Temple."

Finally able to give himself to this new philosophy, Paul asked James, "Why, then, do you not seek out Romans to join you in this? Is this Kingdom of God only for Jews?" James answered, "We are Jews. Our lives are spent as faithful Jews. While we welcome those from all parts of the world into our circles, as Jews we prefer to speak to Jews. For most of our people the Romans are the enemy. Though Jesus tells us to love our enemies, if we were to take many of them into our circles and escape persecution, many of our less advanced followers would suspect that we had made a pact with the Romans and had compromised our integrity. I need not tell you of all men, Paul, the danger of our current situation."

Hearing this, Paul was willing to share the information he had as a citizen of the Empire about the workings of Rome in order to help the Christian church survive its persecution by the Romans. Whereas once

Paul's political ambitions had caused many arrests and executions by Rome, the information and knowledge gained through those same ambitions aided the survival of the early church.

Nonetheless, word eventually reached Herod Agrippa that Saul of Tarsus had returned to Jerusalem and was now working with the Christians, presumably against the Roman occupation. It is true that many of the early Christians were Zadokites or Sicarii, militant radicals who were committed to the violent overthrow of the Roman government. While James, Simeon, and the others preached against violence, claiming that "he who lives by the sword shall die by the sword", conditions in Jerusalem were getting worse by the day.

The Roman officials had determined that the various sub-sects of Judaism, in fact all except the "establishment" Pharisees, were a danger and a threat to the security of the Empire's Judean provinces. Wholesale arrests and executions without trial were now commonplace. Rome had commandeered the Temple treasuries and stores of grain, and most of the Jews living in Jerusalem and the province of Judea were near starvation. Taxes, both from the Romans and the Temple, were increased, and tax rebellions often erupted spontaneously in the streets whenever taxes were to be collected.

Not surprisingly, many of the Christian church (who did not ever embrace the term "Christian" but preferred the more acceptable "Nazorite" or "Nazorean" title) whose sympathies were toward the radical or militant grew impatient with the non-violent approach advocated by James. Many Jews wanted action rather than insight, and broke with the sect.

By this time, Paul had become a wise and trusted member of the Christian community, and was deputized by Simeon and James to try to bring these dissidents to a more spiritual perspective. Paul, in conference with these rebels, found that they had joined the Nazorean movement looking for the Messiah, having heard that Jesus was indeed the leader of the rebellion foretold in prophecy. They had heard that Jesus overcame death at the hands of the Romans, and expected this Jesus to lead an army and restore the rightful king to the Throne of Israel.

Their disillusionment came when they realized that not only was this new movement of a less worldly cast, but that Jesus the supposed Messiah was not even in Jerusalem and had no interest whatsoever in leading an army. Paul was able to pacify these people by claiming that Jesus was indeed the Messiah, chosen by God to lead the people to a new freedom, but that the freedom was of the soul, not of the body. When pressed to make his claims tangible, Paul openly confessed his former life as Saul of Tarsus, spy and betrayer of the Christians. Paul claimed that it was an encounter with Jesus "in spirit" that brought about the transformation that made him an advocate for Jesus's way.

Paul soon found that this argument had great power, and that by painting Jesus as the true and only Messiah, leader of a spiritual rather than a political revolution, the name of Jesus became a rallying cry for non-violent resistance to Rome. In addition, by telling his personal tale of transformation, Paul began to receive adulation, progressing to the point where Paul had more followers and adherents—mostly drawn from the more radical movements—than did James and Simeon.

Although James was willing to accept that Paul was able to quell military action among the more radical members of the church, he resented Paul's emphasis on the personality of Jesus. "How else can I achieve such results with these warlike men but in the name of Jesus?" Paul protested. James replied, "My brother does not wish himself to be put forward as a leader of any movement. He is no more the Messiah than you or I. Each of us has within ourselves the divinity to lead our people to the Kingdom, and one man is not greater than another."

This schism between James and Paul grew, and despite the efforts of James to curb the "personality cult" that Paul was developing, Paul continued to preach in the name of a man he had only seen once in the flesh and once in a spiritual state. Unable to figure out how to deal with the success of Paul in bringing more members into the sect but with the distortions Paul promulgated, James went to Masada to consult with Jesus.

# CHAPTER TWENTY

# The Fall of Jerusalem

SOON AFTER THE DEATH of Miriam, word came to Masada that several of the deacons of the church in Jerusalem had been executed, not by crucifixion or stoning, which were the forms used when either the Sanhedrin or the King had condemned a Jew, but by beheading, which could only be a sentence and execution committed by the Romans. Realizing that the Romans had decided that the Christians were a threat and would be persecuting them more actively, Joseph of Arimithea recommended that Mary and her three children should leave Masada.

Jesus, through his clairvoyance, had "seen" that no place in Judea, Galilee, Idumaea, Samaria, or any of the other Semitic provinces would be safe for Jews in the times to come. After much prayer and discussion, Jesus determined that Joseph should take Mary, their sons Nathaniel and Yusef and their daughter Miriam out of the country. Joseph had planned to settle in a mystery-school community which he had financed in the southern part of Gaul, in what would now be southeastern France. Mary and the grown children were preparing for their journey when James arrived from Jerusalem.

Jesus listened to the claims James made against Paul, and recommended that for the good of all involved, Paul should be sent to Damascus, where the Christian community was growing larger and was freer from both politics and persecution. Paul, having grown up in Damascus, Jesus said, would be more effective there since he knew the local ways, and there was no danger of him causing political trouble.

Jesus offered to his beloved brother the freedom of passage to Gaul with his family, but James told Jesus, "It is more important for me to continue what you began in Jerusalem. Even if I die there, it is my life's work. I gather that is why, my brother, you choose to stay here in Masada."

Jesus said, "You know I fear not death, and there is great need of my teaching here. Our land will soon be no more, and it is best that you and I stay here to guide our people from the land, just as Moses and Aaron led our ancestors to this land but never lived within its borders." They spoke of Jude, who traveled throughout Asia Minor, setting up communities of healers and teachers, and of Peter, who, according to reports, had traveled through Egypt and ended up in Rome. Jesus showed James letters from Peter, written in code, which told of Peter's exploits in bringing the teachings of Jesus to the center of the Roman Empire itself. Jesus also spoke of the high spiritual and healing advancements of the community at Masada, and told James that, as the city was on top of a mountain in a place of great physical power, it would be a mistake for Jesus to leave.

Mary and the children sailed with Joseph, and James returned to Jerusalem. Jesus remained at Masada, living a most modest life with his sister Ruth for companionship. With little interest in the intrigues of politics but sensing a need for the continuity of his teachings, Jesus—who had formerly eschewed the idea of setting his philosophy into writing—decided that he would write a small document that would be the foundation of what would become the Christian church in order to prevent such distortions as Paul's from changing his message. Ruth would help him write this book. (It is perhaps worth noting that the other siblings of Jesus, Miriam, Joses, and Simon, who were also in residence at Masada, returned to Jerusalem with James. There Miriam married Simeon, the chief deacon.)

Back in Jerusalem, James informed Paul that Jesus had recommended that Paul travel to Damascus, where he would be of greater service. In James's absence, Paul had begun to write letters to the distant outposts of the movement "in the name of Jesus", a deed that caused James to accuse Paul of attempting to take over the administration of the church. Paul retorted, "James, you are a wise and gifted man, but you do not know how the people in these outer lands think and behave. Yes, you have traveled widely and have read many books of a spiritual nature, but you don't understand that many in these remote towns are not Jews. They come from mixed backgrounds as do I. For your Kingdom of God to reach these people, they must have a god-figure mightier than their old gods or they will not ever believe the message of Jesus."

Tired, angry, and frustrated, James told Paul that, before going to Damascus, Paul should go to Masada to speak and study with Jesus himself. Paul blanched at this. He recalled that Jesus had appeared to him on the road to Damascus and was afraid to face Jesus in the flesh. Paul left the room, went to his lodgings, packed his belongings, and left for Damascus immediately. When James heard this news, he was angrier still with Paul, but Jesus appeared to James in a vision, assuring him that "If Paul speaks the truth, there is nothing you or I can do to inhibit him. If he speaks lies, no one will believe him. Leave him alone to find his own way. Better he is on our side than against us."

While in Jerusalem, Paul found a young man named Timothy who was also a student of James and Simeon, and was also homosexual. (It should be noted that the Essenes and early Christians did not condemn monogamous homosexual relationships, as long as they were founded on genuine love and respect. As such, the early Christians held all of their members to the same standards regardless of sexual orientation.) Paul and Timothy traveled to Damascus, and began to teach in the community headed by Zechariah.

Without going into great detail, suffice it to say that the rivalry between James and Paul continued for many years. Wherever Paul and Timothy went, they converted many gentiles first to Judaism, and then to the particular brand of Judaism that Paul now openly called "Christianity". Paul's intellect, his personal charisma, the story of his conversion, and his keen awareness of political segregations made him an ideal "recruiter" to bring the works and teachings of Jesus to the gentiles. The problem he encountered repeatedly was that the Jews of Damascus did not necessarily want to include gentiles in the movement. Driven as he was by his new-found zeal, Paul found that he was never welcome in strictly Jewish circles, and so he turned to the gentiles, which made him even more unwelcome among the Jews.

Zechariah of Damascus eventually wrote to James asking that Paul be removed, and a suitable post was found for Paul in Antioch. This was to be the beginning of a long and patchy career that is rather well detailed in the Acts of the Apostles, although that document is biased in favor of Paul and omits his rival James almost entirely. It is not necessary to relate all of Paul's adventures in this present book, but his road eventually led him to Rome, where he encountered a well-established church that had been developed by Peter. By that time, Peter and his followers had set down a number of books that outlined the life and philosophy of Jesus, and the teachings of Paul were clearly at odds with the teachings of Peter. The next chapter discusses these differences and their implications.

In Jerusalem, persecution of the Christians continued, and in 66 C.E. a number of unrelated sects actually armed themselves and attempted, almost successfully, to overthrow the Romans. By this time, most of the original Christians had fled the city, but a small, influential and courageous group remained, led by James and Simeon and his wife Miriam, the sister of James and Jesus. As the revolution spread and it appeared that the rebels were about to be slaughtered, a meeting of Christians led by James was broken into by the Roman armies and, taking their gathering for an insurrectional group, the soldiers slaughtered all in the house. James, the brother of Jesus, was the first one killed.

In Masada, this news saddened Jesus. While Jesus knew that his work and teaching was spreading, he felt the loss of his beloved brother, coupled with the separation from his wife and children, very deeply. He and Ruth suspended the daily work on their book to mourn the death of James with the community.

Word came then to Masada that, although Simeon and Miriam were desperately trying to hold the church in Jerusalem together, the Roman armies were systematically decimating all Jews in the city. Jesus appeared to Miriam and Simeon in a vision, sending them to take over the church in Antioch that had been abandoned by Paul. As Simeon and Miriam left Jerusalem with their followers, the Roman soldiers began to destroy the Temple. During the ensuing battle, most of the Jews remaining in

Jerusalem were slaughtered and almost all of the Temple buildings were pulled down.

Jerusalem, which had been a prized possession of the Roman Empire, had always been a source of trouble. No Roman proconsul was ever able to control the strong-willed, independent Jews of the city; no puppet king was ever given enough authority to curb the Jews' love of freedom from oppression; and despite the corruption and greed that ruined the Temple from the inside, the Romans were never able to sway the Jews from their worship of their own God. The Roman "problem" of Jerusalem, in fact all of Judea, was finally settled by destroying the city itself and running all of the Jews out of the province, as Jesus had foretold.

By 68 C.E. the only stronghold of Jews left in all of Judea was the walled city of Masada. In 70 C.E., a group of Zealots overthrew the Roman military garrison and closed themselves and the city off from the Romans. For almost three years Masada was under siege from the Roman troops, and when the Romans finally entered in 73 C.E., they found all of the inhabitants of the city dead. Only a handful of women and children survived, and they were found cowering in an underground cave.

It is still a mystery today how the Jews of Masada were able to hold the Romans at bay for such a long time. Some of their ability to survive came from the fact that the mystery school in which Jesus did most of his final teaching and healing provided the spiritual heart and soul of the city, making its inhabitants unafraid of death and aware that the true life of the spirit, the indwelling God, survives with or without a physical vessel. What appeared to the Romans to be a mass suicide was in fact the residents of Masada willingly and effortlessly releasing themselves from physical form.

Jesus himself left physical form in 70 C.E. He was soon followed by his sister Ruth. Outside the city of Masada, his teachings were spreading throughout the known world. The book that he and Ruth wrote in Masada was destroyed during the final Roman attack on that city.

Mary of Bethany and her children survived in Gaul, where to this day she, in a transmuted form as Mary Magdalene (La Madeleine), is still worshipped. The descendants of Yusef, Nathaniel, and Miriam, the children of Jesus and Mary, were able to trace their bloodlines for at least three centuries, for at the Council of Nicaea in 325 C.E., two "bishops" from the Marian church in the south of Gaul made a case for certain facts about their ancestors to be included in the canonical literature. (See the next chapter.)

Paul and Peter both ended up in Rome, and both were executed there. Jude traveled through the Far East, establishing churches as far as India, and finally settled in Alexandria in Egypt. Through all of this time, many people, including Jude, began to write their recollections of Jesus and of his teachings. Paul, of course, wrote many, many letters outlining policies, many of which survive to this day in the New Testament. Peter and James wrote equally as many letters, of which only a letter from each is included in the New Testament, along with a single letter from Jude condemning Paul. Why this should be so can best be explained from the perspective of the Council of Nicaea in 325 C.E., convened at the request of the first "Christian" Emperor, Constantine.

# CHAPTER TWENTY-ONE

# The Distortions of Paul

I N OUR FINAL CHAPTER TO THIS BOOK, it is time to explain why so many of the statements about the historical Jesus stated herein are at odds with those in the four Gospels and the Acts of the Apostles as well as the various Epistles that follow. It may come as a surprise to many readers that the "divinity" of Jesus was not actually determined until the year 325 C.E., at the Council of Nicaea. Between the time of Jesus and that year, the Roman Empire crumbled, and although it was still in some form of existence, it was not the same empire as it was, and was no longer dominated by Rome itself. The emperor Constantine was originally a member of a Mithraic sun-worshipping cult. It is said that before going into battle, a vision of Jesus came to him, saying, "In my name you will conquer". Constantine rode into battle under a flag with a cross on it, and won the day.

The truth of the matter is that by the end of the third century, Christianity had gone from a persecuted fringe sect to a major power. In order for Constantine to rule over the many lands then contained in the Roman

Empire, he had to reckon with many of the organized churches, each of which used different texts that were at variance with each other.

The first history to be written about Jesus was what is now known as the Gospel of Thomas (Didymus), which survives in barely altered form. This, of course, was the work of Jesus's brother Jude. Peter made an attempt to write down his recollections of Jesus, but was unschooled and his document was clumsy and artless, if heartfelt. These two books, that of Peter and that of Jude, were the only ones written by people who actually knew Jesus. The book that Jesus and Ruth wrote in Masada is lost, but following this chapter is a rough approximation of its introduction, read from the Akashic Records.

Most of the books that were written after the passing of Jesus into spirit and the fall of Masada were at best third-hand, based on oral histories gained from those who spoke to someone who knew someone who actually knew Jesus. The document that pre-dates the Gospel of Mark is the result of combining one of these histories with a rough copy of Peter's book. Jude's book went through several radical transformations as it was translated, so that by the time it became the Gospel of John it would have been unrecognizable to its author. (A separate line of Eastern Christianity managed to preserve a more authentic copy that surfaced in Russia prior to the discovery of an older text at Nag Hammadi.)

Before these books were widely distributed, however, the letters of Paul, Peter, and James circulated, and between Paul and the other two differing portraits of Jesus grew. While James and Peter shared a common vision of Jesus that concentrated mostly on his teaching and healing, Paul wrote for gentiles who had no knowledge of Jewish law.

In each of his letters that comprise the Epistles of Paul of the New Testament, Paul creates a radically different Jesus based on the subjects to whom the letters were written, just as Paul tries to justify himself to those groups. The multi-cultural Paul creates a Hebraic Jesus in his letter to the Hebrews, a Roman demigod in his letter to the Romans, a mystical Eastern potentate in his letter to the Ephesians, and so on.

In order to bring the essentially Jewish teachings of Jesus to a wider, non-Jewish audience, Paul unashamedly incorporated figures and details from the mythologies of the cultures he addressed. It must be remembered that Paul sincerely wanted to convey what he perceived as the teachings of Jesus in a form that would be understandable to many cultures, so as the biography of Jesus was passed around orally and in Paul's teachings, the life of Jesus absorbed many mythical dimensions.

In order to reach cultures that would find Jesus's concept of an In-dwelling God too abstract or mystical (and Paul was no mystic himself), Paul was forced to raise Jesus to the level of a demi-God. Many of the healings of Jesus were exaggerated in order to compete with the wonders worked by other gods in other lands. Greek and Roman demi-gods were generally sired by the gods consorting with mortals, so for his Greek and Roman audiences Paul had Miriam impregnated by Yahweh himself. In addition, many Eastern cultures would only accept a god of virgin birth.

All of this would be acceptable if only Paul had not started making his own rules for conduct and behavior which were often at odds with the rules and laws taught by Jesus. It must also be said that Paul is not solely responsible for all that now exists in the Epistles. Each time they were written and circulated, scribes and bishops added those details which they deemed necessary, so that what we now read as Paul's letters are perhaps half Paul and half later writers.

Paul, however, is responsible for most of the details in the book called Acts, which details his travels and missions and almost totally negates the work done by James and Jude. Rather than glorify those two, with whom Paul bitterly disagreed, Paul chose to attribute many of their actions and deeds to Peter, with whom Paul had little contact and, consequently, high regard.

It was not until Peter and Paul met briefly in Rome before they were both executed that Peter was able to express his dissatisfaction with Paul's letters. By then, both were old men and were willing to forgive each other in the face of impending death, for there was a purge of Christians in Rome as great as the Roman purge of Jews in Judea.

It is ironic that the Roman Empire, which tried to systematically eradicate the sect that followed Jesus, would, through the political compromise of Constantine, turn into the official guardian of Christianity, albeit in a Pauline form.

Paul's insistence that Jesus was sired by Yahweh forced him to then send Jesus back to Heaven after his resurrection, for the image of a Divine Christ was at odds with the historical Jesus who lived into his seventies.

More importantly, as Paul moved into a more and more Roman-dominated world and greater numbers of Roman citizens converted to

Christianity, he found it increasingly difficult to lay the blame for the execution of Jesus upon the Roman Empire, so he shifted more and more of the blame onto the Jews themselves.

When the letter now known as the Epistle of Jude was circulated among the young churches attempting to discredit the teachings of Paul, Paul began to discredit Jude, eventually shifting Jude's role from a loving brother to that of "Judas Iscariot", the betrayer of Jesus (a figure without much historicity).

Since there were blood descendants of Jesus living in Gaul, it became increasingly troublesome to Paul to think that they could attempt to stop his progress, so be began to teach that Jesus never married, and that his circle did not include any women at all, save Mary of Bethany. Her legend proved so difficult to Paul that he debased the loving marriage she and Jesus had by turning her into the reformed prostitute Mary of Magdala.

In short, what Paul did was take a real human being whom he had encountered and transform Jesus into a mythological figure. While Paul did this knowingly in order to spread "the word", he truly felt that he was following the teachings of Jesus. In reality, however, Paul's attempt backfired over the course of history. Where Jesus spent his entire life teaching that every man and woman has within himself or herself a part of God and that the God-self or Christ-self can be realized while in human form, Paul spread a notion that only Jesus was "the Son of God" to the exclusion of all other mortals.

Jesus meant to be an example to others that death should not be feared; Paul turned him into an angelic being who had a special dispensation against death by virtue of his divine parentage while the rest of humanity was doomed to suffer and die. Through a Hellenistic appropriation, Paul was able to tell his listeners that Jesus would redeem them from death after death if they only believed in his name. All of this may have succeeded in bringing more converts into the fold, after which Paul may have been able to truly teach and initiate the faithful, but such a mission was always cut short by Paul's need to keep moving.

The long-standing Christian movement in Rome, led by Peter, was closer in all respects to the teachings of Jesus, but because the Roman purge was so effective and the sect was driven so far underground, most of the Petrine writings of that era were lost or destroyed. Today we have as a record only what the Romans themselves wrote about the very

Christians they were trying to destroy.

To absolve Paul of some of the responsibility of the "personality cult" surrounding Jesus, it must be admitted that such a development is inevitable. Such cults developed around Mohammed, Confucius, Gautama Buddha, and, in this century, similar developments are beginning to surround Gandhi and Martin Luther King.

In the two centuries after Peter and Paul were executed, the Christian movement grew in strength and numbers, and eventually the Christians moved "above ground". For these public sects, texts were needed to substantiate the life and teachings of Jesus, and by the time the gospels of Mark, Matthew, Luke, and John were widely circulated, they were several times removed from the realities they purported to represent and contained a hodge-podge of myths picked up in dozens of lands. (Matthew and Luke are both based on Mark, which is why those three gospels are at odds with the "John" gospel, which derives from Jude's memoirs.)

When Constantine, who had embraced the burgeoning Christian movement to avoid going to battle with them (even though he did not actually abandon his Mithraism for the teachings of Jesus), sought to unify all of the warring factions within the Christian church, he summoned all of the leading bishops to Nicaea to determine the doctrine and dogma of the official church of his empire. As we have seen with the various doctrines of Paul, by 325 C.E. the number of texts and, therefore, images of Jesus was beyond count. Each bishop brought a retinue of clerics, and each one of these brought documents. As mentioned before, two direct descendants of Jesus and Mary came to the conference, albeit not at the behest of the Emperor, and so were not allowed into the actual council itself. In fact, some of the most radical theologians of the time were also not part of the official council.

As a result, there were two Councils of Nicaea, one official and one unofficial. Among the matters "settled" by the official council were: Jesus was of divine, virgin birth and was, therefore, of equal status with God the Father; Jesus was indeed the only Son of God; Jesus was never married and, therefore, had no offspring; Jesus ascended into Heaven soon after his resurrection.

The Council itself also decided to remove all mention of reincarnation from the official scriptures; they sanctioned as a holy rite the Eucharist, commemorating the Passover Seder held before the crucifixion as a symbolic sharing of the flesh and blood of the Messiah (a concept that appealed to Constantine's Mithraism); they established Sunday as the Sabbath day instead of Saturday (another nod to Constantine's sun-worship); and they agreed to codify their resolutions into a creed. This creed, known today as the Nicene Creed, is still used to pledge solidarity with the "official" church and, as such, has been used through the centuries for exclusion from official ranks.

This was the official business, hotly debated. Other issues dealt with the theory of dualism put forth by Arius, which stated that flesh and spirit were separate and not consubstantial (an issue causing much turmoil in the hierarchy of the church). The dualists were ruled to be heretics. Most importantly, the unofficial business also included the clandestine assembly of an official canon of scriptures and epistles, so that the newly organized "state church" could standardize its beliefs.

The committee assigned this task pored over all of the documents presented, and immediately rejected any but those which supported the agenda that the council had adopted. This meant that the gospels written by Peter and Jude were rejected as heresies, and the heavily edited versions of Matthew, Mark and Luke were admitted as "official" tales of the life of Jesus. A strong and influential faction lobbied for the inclusion of the mystical gospel of John, and to appease them, it was included.

Peter and his authentic, if Romanized, form of Christianity was the biggest loser at this conference, since the distortions of the truth perpetrated by Paul, as well as his own codes for conduct and living, were adopted as canonical, with only a very small nod to Peter, James, and Jude. In fact, since the First Council of Nicaea, the New Testament was assembled much as it stands today.

A quick survey of the contents of the New Testament shows that Paul is represented more heavily than any other author. Yet along with the gospel of "John" was added another book by "John" which, if properly read, is a key to spiritual enlightenment: The Book of Revelation. Unfortunately, this is a document that was secretly passed among the churches in a kind of code, so that the Romans who might get their hands on it would be baffled. Even in that coded form which has come down to us today, it is a description of what happens as the chakras (the "Seven Seals") are opened during a spiritual initiation. It is not, as generally believed, a book of prophecy, although it touches, in obscure symbology, the Roman persecution of the Christians. (Appendix Three gives a brief key to interpreting this most confusing of documents.)

Another editorial policy established after the Council was coordinating the gospels with Old Testament prophecies, specifically Isaiah, so that it could be made clear that Jesus was indeed the Messiah predicted by the prophets of old. In truth, those prophets were pointing the way to the same process taught by Jesus that led to a personal, spiritual enlightenment, in which every soul could awaken to its own divinity.

In removing the family relationship of Jesus and Mary, their descendants were therefore disinherited of any spiritual or temporal legacy or prominence in the Church. Moreover, by adopting the misogynistic rules of conduct of Paul, women were excluded from becoming celebrants in the newly organized church. If the reader recalls the way the Essenes conducted themselves in this regard, it is clear that the Council of Nicaea and its subsequent "reforms" undid nearly all that the Essenes stood for.

Despite all of these distortions, upon which thousands upon thousands of lives have been lost, the basic teachings of Jesus are still discernible in the scriptures. So strong and simple were his teachings that millions are still inspired by his words, thoughts, and deeds. A time has now dawned when people around the world are able to receive the truer facts and statements about his life, and accept Jesus as a mortal who achieved divinity while in earthly form rather than a divine being who descended to Earth.

It is hoped that this book does not alter or change the faith of those who still admire and follow the teachings of Jesus. The reason it has been put forth is to make women and men aware that no matter who one is or in what time one may live, it is always possible to discover the Indwelling God that Jesus spoke of and realized; to reinforce the mission of Jesus: to be an example of what humanity can become. Since bodies are conceived, are lived in, and "die" when they are of no earthly use and since the spirit lives on eternally, the spirit that was Jesus during the time from 4 B.C.E. to 70 C.E. is still among us, and will offer guidance and inspiration to anyone who genuinely and humbly seeks it from him who is a brother and fellow seeker of the ultimate truth.

*"You shall know the truth*
*and the truth shall make you free."*

# PART THREE

## Appendices

# Appendix I

# Introduction to
## *The Teachings of Jesus*

*(The following document is an approximation of the introduction to the book written by Jesus and his sister Ruth in the fortress of Masada between the years 66-70 C.E.)*

I, Y'SHUA BEN YUSEF OF GALILEE, writing with my beloved sister Ruth, offer this book as my own words and teachings. There are in the world many today who pretend to teach in my name, but they are not my students. Many who pretend to come in my name have never met me in the flesh. Many lies and false teachings are being spread in my name.

This book, which I set down only after long prayer and contemplation, is the sum of my learning. I write it so that after I leave this plane my teachings may go on unquestioned. Thus I will leave this book in a place where no rust nor rot may come to it, but in a place to be reached by the mind and the soul.

Mayhap the scroll that my sister writes upon shall perish, but there is a place where all the deeds of men are written, and may be read by those who learn how to read such books. This place is in the Kingdom of Heaven, and the Kingdom of Heaven is within our minds.

All my life's work has been based on three ideas: all creatures on Earth and in Heaven are created by the greatest God, to whom we owe our lives and our common origins; what appears to be reality on earth is only an illusory manifestation of spirit; and there are no such things as fear or death, there is only love.

It was love that brought all creatures into existence, such great love that could only belong to the great Father and Mother of all things seen and unseen. For the greatest God created all things to be of love like Itself; God created nor form nor matter, nor anything earthly. Earth is not God's domain. God gave Earth to men so that they could learn to be equal with God.

In the most ancient of times, before the planets and the suns were created, all creatures of Earth were part of God. Yet within God there was a conflict so deep that God shattered Itself into countless fragments, so that these fragments of God were all one and the same God, yet in myriad parts. Some of these parts brought into being flesh and matter, a world where creatures were born, devoured, and died, only to be transformed into ever new and more complicated forms.

Those who created this world took dominion over it, and saw that all creatures in the world were given life and freedom. The creators of these worlds, who had split from the unending God, so fell in love with their world that they desired to join it. Yet that world was in such a greatly different form that they could not inhabit it, unless they became form itself.

Hence, that which is without form and is pure mind, pure spirit, slowed itself down and became what is now termed flesh. So great was the love of those angelic beings for the world that they took on its form, and in time forgot who they were. I was one of those beings.

Great was the curse put upon themselves by taking on form and forgetting that they were but part of the greatest God, parts which in themselves encompassed all that could be imagined. For countless centuries they lived upon the earth, turning their backs on the divine parts of themselves, and becoming flesh.

When seen from the eyes of the flesh only, this world now seems as real as it did to them, but when seen with the inner eyes, the eyes of God, the flesh and all things can be seen for what they are.

For in the Domain of God there is not matter, nor flesh, nor time, but only love and endless creation.

Hence it can be said that the Kingdom of God did not ever cease to be, but has always existed for those who choose to live therein. Yet on this earth, the Kingdom of God seems far away. If your eyes are not trained to see any things but those of matter, there may be no Kingdom of God at all.

I have spent my life teaching that all that the body's eyes see is illusion, and what the spirit knows is the truth. Within the system of the world all things have existence and form because they are created of the mind of God, yet forget their own divine nature.

To be certain of the divine nature of all things is as simple as waking from a dream, for that is what it is. Through time there have been many who have awakened from that dream, and have tried to tell their fellows that they are only dreaming. Yet the dreamer does not want to have a dream shattered. It was therefore seen fit to destroy the speaker of truth to perpetuate the dream. Alas, those who fight and kill to perpetuate the dream of illusion are doomed to endless rounds of repetition of that selfsame illusion, until once again they are awakened to their divine, true natures.

I am one who, while born as a man, have awakened to my true nature as a child of God. It has been my life's work to bring others to a waking state. I have felt the limitations and the pleasures of the flesh, and have returned to this life for one last time to taste again of its pleasures, for pleasures there are in this world. Who would not want to enjoy a pleasant, brief dream, even knowing throughout that it is but a dream?

Yet beyond this dream is the reality of our natures, our common God-hood. And as all things are made of the mind of God, all things seen and unseen are created of the same mind, and are therefore united in divinity. How, then, can men oppress their fellow men without doing harm to themselves?

I write this in a city that is soon to be under siege from my brothers. Many have wondered how I can sit still in this city and allow this to happen without taking up arms, as others are doing. This is not my way, though it is the way of many men. My way is not yet for all men to follow. I stand only to point the direction to reality. I am only a guide, for a guide may point the traveler in the right direction, but does not make the traveler's journey for him.

Soon I will give up the limits of the flesh to return to my true state, yet I will not regain my place in the vast fabric that is the mind of God until all my brothers and sisters make the same journey that I have made. It is necessary for all who have made the decision to inhabit this world to realize their true selves. Through countless ages of living and dying, fighting, striving, we have forgotten who we are, beings of light whom men call angels or spirit beings.

Around you all the time are beings of spirit, some in flesh, some not. Those in flesh often are not aware of the spirit, just as the spirit beings are not always aware of those in flesh, yet when those barriers break down, as when a glass ceases to reflect the image of the watcher to reveal another face behind the glass, we all have moments where we glimpse our true selves.

When a spirit being becomes flesh, it enters through pain and blood to the world of the body. When it dies, in pain and blood, it returns to the nature of spirit. When the first ones who became flesh lived in bodies, they forgot that they were ever beings of spirit, and were asleep for thousands upon thousands of years.

A time is upon us when, as beings of spirit, we are becoming aware of ourselves again. What we have brought into being is a world where we may learn more quickly of our true natures while in bodies. Hence, the body has become a learning tool, through which we may realize our true natures. A life spent in service to others, knowing that all are a part of the great mind of God, is a life that brings one closer to reunion with God.

We are all like the sheep of a flock who have lost their way, and find themselves in a strange land where there is no grass to graze nor water to drink, and we dare not run one way or another for fear we will lose our lives. I am like the shepherd who, when finding those stray sheep, simply turns them around the next hill to find grass and water in abundance.

There are those of whom I wrote that look to me as more than shepherd, who wish to make of me a king or a monarch, to raise me above my brothers and sisters. That is why I stay here, away from such men. For through my words and deeds I shall merely point you the way home, take you around the nearest hill, so that you may graze in the Kingdom of God. I am no more king than the lowest shepherd in the field, yet the shepherd in the field is no less divine than I.

In times past, when men were awakened to their true natures yet turned their eyes away, our ancestor Moses wrote down in the law what all men should have known without being told. The law was given as a guidepost to those who were lost. Through time there are many guideposts, if the traveler has the sense to heed them. No one is so lost that there are not many guides to point the way. Yet many are deaf to the words and blind to the gestures of the guides. Were this not so, there would be no need for the guides at all, for those who are lost would find their way of themselves.

Yet since this is not so, my life has been spent as but one of many guides. I point the way for you into your own heart, where lies your home. To that home I shall soon return, and many will follow me.

Like a traveler who is so long and so far from home that he does not remember the look of places nor the faces of others, there is still within each being who lives a deep longing and remembrance for the home of the Father and the Mother.

Who is your father? Not he who sired you, for he is your brother. Who is your mother? Not she who carried and birthed you, for she is your sister. Your Father is God and your Mother is God. On Earth in one life you may be father to one who is your mother in another life, yet in the Kingdom of God all are equal in might and wisdom.

Many looked to me to destroy the law and the prophets. All my life I have lived by the law and the prophets, when those laws did not violate the spirit. Yet the law states to love your neighbor as yourself, to which I add, you must love your enemy as yourself, for your enemy is yourself, made of the same mind of God. How, then, can you be enemy to yourself, or neighbor to yourself? Be only love, for love is all there is.

No greater love has the shepherd for his sheep, no greater love has the mother for her babe than the love that brought us into being by allowing Itself to separate into so many parts. Yet within each part of God which is our selves, there is also the whole of God. For God is not substance, which can be shattered, but God is the divine love that can only be multiplied.

In the world there is strife and tribulation, because we are divided against ourselves. To take arms against a supposed enemy would be taking arms against ourselves. To wound and kill your fellow man is to prolong reunion with God, for he who takes arms and kills thinks that death brings an end. To bring death to a brother or sister only prolongs your sleep on Earth.

For it is true that my body was taken and put to death, but I have gone beyond death to regain my life, merely to show you that death is not to be feared. Those who truly teach in my name know that the spirit lives eternally and outside time, and is perfect in form.

Those who heal in the name of God are simply restoring the perfection that is already manifest in the spirit realm, which is the true Kingdom of God. The body is but the greatest of schools. Who would not go to a school to learn better how to live, but who would not willingly leave the school behind when those lessons are learned?

There will come a day when time is no more, when fear and hatred are no more, and the world will cease to exist, its need for existence no longer a matter of necessity. When I see who my true Mother and Father is, I am filled with enough love to bring such a world to an end. Yet until every woman and man has made that decision to regain the divine nature, I will stay with you in spirit to be your shepherd and guide.

These are the only words that I can teach you, brothers and sisters. All teachings else are but elaborations and illustrations of these principles.

Though times may seem to threaten you, though oppression and cruelty may end your life on earth, think of all these things as lessons you have set for yourself, that you may hasten to become once again what you were born to be long before time.

Blessings to all who simply and humbly seek to know the truth.

# APPENDIX II

# *The Akhnaton–Moses Doctrine*

*[This doctrine was drawn up by the pharaoh Akhnaton and the prophet Moses while Moses was the leader of the Jews in Egypt. It is a summary of the conclusions drawn jointly by these two seers and duly recorded before the Jews left Egypt.]*

THERE IS ONLY ONE GOD, and this is the God of all peoples. We, the Jews, are in supposed captivity and slavery by the people of the Pharaoh of all Egypt, the great Akhnaton. Yet where God enters no slavery can come. Moses the Jew and Akhnaton set their hands to this document in the city of Amarna under the watchful eye of the all-seeing God.

That there is to be no war between our peoples is because the all-seeing, all-knowing eye of God watches all people as one. There are those in the world who would enslave, who would conquer, but only God can conquer and God is the force of love.

Is it not love that brings into the world new life? Was it not love that brought us into the world? Was it not the wisdom of love that led the people of Israel into the arms of Egypt, where two prophets would meet to share the same vision?

Though to the world the Jews are the slaves of the Pharaoh Akhnaton, we two peoples are bound by the love that created us. Know, peoples of the world, that if the Jews and the Egyptians can share a God, it is the God of the whole world, and will bring enlightenment to all who believe in this God.

There are many gods in the world now, and these gods want blood and sacrifice. These are false gods, for any god that demands tribute is no true god. The true god demands only devotion.

No man has seen the face of God, for God has no face. Yet all men have seen the faces of God, for God is in all people. Deep devotion and prayer will bring the devotee into a realm where sight is clear, and the faces of God can be seen in the faces of all men.

An initiation is needed for all men to gain this sight, but the sight does not clear until the soul leaves the body at death. Yet through prayer the soul can detach from the body and see many wonders which are in the world. All men are the same when seen in this sight, for all are luminous beings, brighter and more wondrous than any sun, moon or stars that light the heavens.

The light of the heavens is the face of God. The shining of the sun and moon upon the earth are the light of God. The love in the hearts of men is the heart of God. The face that looks upon the other in love is the face of God.

God has many names but no name. The sight of man is limited, so God becomes only what man can see. Yet man, even in the best sight, without eyes, cannot see all of what God is.

God is found in the hollows of the hills. God is found in the depths of the ocean. There is no place where God is not.

The man who tries to escape the sight of God might well try to hide from himself. There is no place where God is not.

The sight of God sees all things seen and unseen, yet the hand of God acts not, for the hand of God does not touch man. Only when man goes hand in hand with God does the hand of God touch man.

Wonders are possible through the hand of God-in-man, yet no wonders are possible by the hand of man without the hand of God being within the hand of man.

Man has turned his back upon God, yet God will never turn His back upon man.

Man lives now in darkness, and has told himself that he loves the darkness. In the darkness is much evil and treachery conceived and wrought. God sees not the darkness, and God does not see the evil that men do. For in the sight of God there is no evil, there is no sin, only mistakes made by a foolish child who mistakes the darkness for the light.

For the light is life, and the darkness is folly. He who lives in the dark is foolish not to light the lamp that sits at his left hand, yet man does not even see the lamp that sits at his left hand.

He who lives in the light shall not starve or go thirsty, for the hand of God provides for all who hunger and thirst. Yet God has no hands without the hands of men. He who hungers and thirsts will not be given food or drink unless he reaches out his hand and takes from God's offering.

Love is not taken in where there is no love. Love cannot be given to one by diminishing the other. Love multiplies itself when given, and there is no end of love. Where there is no love given, there is no love taken either. He who is without love in his heart sits in the darkness with the light at his back. To see the light, he must turn around, for he sits only in his own shadow, mistaking it for the darkness of night, a night without love.

Turn, o men, from the shadow into the light. It is but a little turning. From the shadows one sees only suffering and darkness, sin and despair, treachery and enslavement. A little turn into the light and one can only see love where once was enmity, charity where once was selfishness, divinity and grace where once was rancor and bitterness, joy and celebration where once was misery and wailing. A little turn, but, o men, how many will make that little turn away from the dark?

For in the dark one sees not the colors that are the light of God-in-man. Brighter than the rainbow are the colors of God-in-man, yet the colors are the same. God-in-man glows even in the dark, yet only the blind and stubborn refuse to see.

Whence comes the gift of vision and prophecy? By a little turn away from darkness into light. Whence comes death and destruction? From a little turning away from the light into darkness.

Many there are who build shelters against the light, and will not let the light enter. Yet the light comes through the smallest crack in any door, no matter how tightly sealed, and once the light enters in, darkness is banished.

Even the darkness of the tomb cannot seal out the light of God, for the corpse is left in the tomb but the spirit goes into the light that is God the Almighty, Maker of all things seen and unseen.

Before God do all differences between men disappear. In the darkness all things are unknown because sight cannot distinguish, and fear rules the dark. In the light all things are known, for all things can be seen clearly. There are no secrets so deep in man that can be hidden from the sight of God-in-man.

It is God-in-man that all men seek to become. To know one's self, one's immortal soul, is to know that part of God which burns like a bright lamp within even the darkest reaches of the body.

For beyond this world are many worlds, and beyond these faces are many faces, and beyond those many faces is the face of one that cannot be seen, the face of God.

Man is the creature of the world that tells stories, and many of these stories are made to conceal the face of God, just as many stories are told to draw the mask away from the face of man. Let us tell those stories that remove the masks of man, and eschew those tales that hide the true face of man.

When a small child is afraid of the dark, a song or a story can calm those fears. When a man is afraid of the dark, there is no song or story that can calm his fears, unless he becomes as a child and hears the songs and stories that show him there is no need to fear anything in the sight of God. In this, the wisdom of the child is more like the Divine than is the foolishness of man.

For the child must be taught to fear death; the child must be taught to fear his fellows; the child must be taught to fear the unknown. So must the man be taught not to fear the dark, not to fear death, not to fear his fellows, but to embrace all as brothers and sisters in the sight of God.

The sight of God is common to all men, but is obscured by the sight of man. The sight of man is a dim light, but the sight of God is at once dimmer than the faintest coal and brighter than the sun. He who looks long at the sun is for a time blind in his daily sight, just as he who looks long with the sight of God becomes blind to his daily, earthly sight.

When the seven seals of light are opened, there is only one sight, the sight of God that sees all as truth. No illusions are there in the sight of God, no hate is there in the mind of God.

From God have we come, and unto God do we return hence.

Let this song be sung in all the far reaches of the Earth.

# Appendix III

# The True Meaning of
## *The Book of Revelation*

ONE FINAL MISCONCEPTION must be set straight by this book before its end. In the New Testament is a book called often *The Revelation of John* or *The Book of Revelation*. It is often mistaken to be a book of prophecy, and has been interpreted to be a prediction of the physical return of Jesus into the world at its destruction.

This mysterious book is written in code, and is a translation of one of the books brought from Egypt by Moses and Aaron. In the form the book took when it was given to them by the Pharaoh Akhnaton, the book was already centuries old. It was brought into the land of Egypt by those who settled that land from the continent known today as Atlantis, from whence many of the earliest Egyptians came.

In that form the book was also centuries old. After the time of Jesus it was rewritten by a monk named Iokanaan (John) who lived in a hermit-like cave near the sea on the Greek island of Patmos. In order to make this ancient document seem relevant to his fellows, John of Patmos made it seem that it had been viewed by him in a dream.

The book itself is of little value as an historical document, but it is of the utmost value as a map to the process often known as enlightenment, awakening or spiritual rebirth.

The path the soul takes through many incarnations of flesh is symbolized by the "fall from grace" of Genesis, and the path through Hell, Gehenna, or the underworld is symbolic of man's path through the material earth.

The enlightenment spoken of in the previous two documents by Jesus and by Akhnaton and Moses can only take place when the divine energy flows into the seven chakras, which are the seven seals of the book. In highly symbolic languages and imagery, the Book of Revelation describes the feelings and visions experienced at the opening of each of the seven chakras.

The images of the book had much meaning in the culture of the times, most of which is lost today. Such knowledge, which can be spoken and written about in the modern age without any shame or secrecy, was considered secret, hidden, or "occult" in earlier times, and, therefore, was of necessity written in a kind of code.

Through the centuries, as with all other books of the Bible, many hands have emended the text. Yet the truth of what can be seen through the various emendations is clear.

Many topical references were made to contemporary politics, to the Roman Empire; many others were made to Jesus Christ. The symbolic meanings of the Roman Empire can be applied to those psychological forces within man that we use to oppress ourselves; the images of Jesus Christ should be taken to mean the Divine Christ, the radiant one who lives within each of us.

For Jesus was not a man who came to earth as the only Son of God to redeem the sins of man through his divine or magical powers. Jesus was a man who actualized his own divinity, and lived his life as an example to all who choose to realize that same Indwelling God.

Through the opening of the seven seals or chakras, everyone can be opened to the Indwelling God or Christ-self that is the true nature of every man and woman. The purpose of being alive in flesh is to actualize the Divinity within. The energies and worlds that exist side by side with the visible world are there to facilitate this process, which is called initiation in much of the preceding book.

The Book of Revelation should be examined as a guidebook to the process of spiritual awakening. It does not predict the end of the physical world in the commonly accepted sense, yet when one undergoes a spiritual enlightenment or awakening, the world of everyday reality ceases to hold any meaning other than a symbolic one, a reality that exists only as a teaching tool.

The greatest sages and teachers of the ancient and modern world choose those forms, like the Book of Revelation, which will speak to their own people in the clearest terms possible. Today when such matters can be discussed openly, the Book of Revelation should be examined as one historical version that attempted to explain and record a process that is the ultimate fate of every being: a return to unity with the Divine One.

The purification of fire and the judgment of Christ are what happens when the sight is opened, as spoken of by Moses and Akhnaton. All that is illusion and dross is burned away by the sight of God, and all that is divine stands in perfect clarity.

Those who read the Book of Revelation as a book of literal prophecy will be disappointed and disillusioned. Those who turn to its pages as a "road map" for spiritual development and initiation will find its wisdom to be outside time and of help and assistance in the process of returning to the True Self.

www.ingramcontent.com/pod-product-compliance
Lightning Source LLC
LaVergne TN
LVHW011232080426
835509LV00005B/455